GW00502168

The Euro for Survival

Entering the Red Zone

Bob Lyddon
Lyddon Consulting Services Limited

Published in May 2018 by
The Bruges Group, 246 Linen Hall, 162-168 Regent Street, London W1B 5TB
www.brugesgroup.com

Follow us on twitter 🐦 @brugesgroup, LinkedIn 🔗 @thebrugesgroup,
Facebook 🔗 The Bruges Group, Instagram 📷 brugesgroup

Bruges Group publications are not intended to represent a corporate view of European
and international developments. Contributions are chosen on the basis of their
intellectual rigour and their ability to open up new avenues for debate.

Contents

Preface: the Euro's battle for survival – entering the red zone

This paper has been commissioned by the Bruges Group as the negotiations about the UK's future relationship with the European Union continue.

At this point the negotiations are being conducted by the UK government on the basis of both a one-to-one dialogue – with the European Commission's negotiators – and latterly one-to-many as well: direct dialogue with the member state heads of government who constitute the European Council.

There is a further angle that the UK government's stance appears to take no note of, which is the many-to-many relationships between the member states and particularly insofar as the future of the Euro impacts them.

The UK's Remainers have successfully inculcated into the Brexit debate here that there has been a Eurozone economic recovery. On the back of that comes the inference that the UK risks on missing out on something good and must maintain the strongest possible economic ties in order to avoid being left out in the cold.

The view of this paper is the opposite. There has been no Eurozone economic recovery. The Eurozone's economic performance is weak and even that is supported on exports to China and a huge cushion of monetary support from the Eurosystem of central banks. The underlying problems are unresolved, central to them being the bad debts owned by the Periphery banking systems and the over-indebtedness of their governments. These problems have been cloaked by the Eurosystem's actions.

But now exports to China are tailing off, interest rates are rising and the Eurosystem has fired off all of its ammunition out of Mr Draghi's bazooka. Two ways forward present themselves:

- Complete centralisation

- Abandon a burning platform

There is an ineluctable logic to proceed towards complete centralisation in terms of what has been done so far, but this logic will turn to horror in the eyes of the citizenry of the Eurozone Centre when the final, few steps to complete centralisation become clear:

1. All EU member states adopt the Euro

2. A single Bank Deposit Compensation Scheme

3. Unification of the Eurosystem into a legal person

4. Harmonisation of the forms of central bank money

5. Mutualisation of government debt

The alternative – to figuratively jump off a burning oil platform and dive into the sea below – may seem attractive by comparison.

The UK's line – to follow a quite different pathway and to get as far away as possible from the impending explosion – is rational, only our own negotiating team don't seem to appreciate the bind that the Eurozone is in and the extreme dangers of our remaining associated with this arrangement.

Executive Summary

There has been no Eurozone economic recovery. The Eurozone's economic performance is weak and even that was supported by buoyant exports to China in 2017 that have now tailed off, and by a huge cushion of monetary support from the Eurosystem.

The underlying problems – exposed in the Eurozone crisis in 2012-13 - are unresolved. These are firstly the bad debts owned by the Periphery banking systems and secondly the over-indebtedness of their governments.

These problems have been cloaked by the Eurosystem's actions under two headings:

1. The ECB's quantitative easing programme known by the name "Asset Purchase Programmes" or "APP" for short, which is now reputed to total €2 trillion;

2. The build-up of overnight loans between the National Central Banks of the Eurozone in the TARGET2 Euro payment system.

These are also inextricably linked to one another: the transaction of a typical APP purchase leads to an increase in loans through TARGET2.

To add to this we have a recent report from the World Bank entitled "Europe needs to boost skills and unshackle firms..." that draws attention to deep-rooted structural issues in the EU economy.

Against this need for reform we can contrast the lending that has been done since 2012 by the European Investment Bank and by its offshoot the European Fund for Strategic Investments. These loans have fulfilled the same objectives as APP, to inject funds into the Eurozone economy, but they have done little to create a foundation for economic growth: they are an example of borrow-and-spend.

It could be thought that the ECB can continue its stimulus ad infinitum, in both time and quantity, but there are several significant forces acting against that.

Firstly the actions of the USA to curtail their own version of APP and to raise interest rates. The mood music amongst central banks is that it is time to taper off their stimulus programmes and allow economies to stand on their own two feet.

Secondly Brexit: the residual member states will have to pay in more money themselves if the EU's programmes are to continue at the same level.

Thirdly all these member states are signatories to the EU Fiscal Stability Treaty – "The Treaty on Stability, Co-ordination and Governance in the EMU" – whereby they have agreed to reduce the ratio of government debt to GDP to 60% by 2030, and to make such adjustments as are needed to spending to take account of additional age-related social costs that may arise up to 2050 i.e. to adjust welfare spending downwards before 2030 so that the 60% ratio can be sustained up until 2050.

Fourthly there is a clear divide in TARGET2 between the lender National Central Banks ("NCBs") and the borrower NCBs, and the lenders see their loans increase steadily, in an arrangement where the loans are secured on the government bonds of the borrower NCB, which is no security at all.

Fifthly it is clear that the bad debts owned in several banking systems are not going down as hoped, and are not being successfully moved into "bad bank" or securitisation structures. Italy is the biggest concern here, because a year ago a securitisation template was established under which the banks would be able to move their NPLs ("Non-Performing Loans") off their books at around 30% of the face value, this being the approximate level to which they had already written them down.

Venture capitalist, however, valued a portfolio of NPLs offered by Unicredit at only slightly above 10% of face value, and this has undermined the viability of the securitisation template: the banks are still holding NPLs at above their market value, but to accept that market value and write the value of the loans down to it would cause the banks to become insolvent.

Lastly the recent Italian election result, which rejects any prolongation of austerity, albeit that even greater austerity would be needed for Italy to comply with the EU Fiscal Stability Treaty, clean up its banks and eliminate its loans in TARGET2.

In the meantime interest rates are actually increasing, if not in the range from overnight to one month but certainly in the 5-10 years range. Since the APP programmes invest in bonds in the 3-15 year maturity range, this rise in interest rates has already caused the Eurosystem to lose value on the bonds, and even a small rise in interest rates causes a very large loss in real money on a portfolio of €2 trillion.

The key issue there is how to taper off APP without actually realising any losses.

These six issues add up to a crisis, in response to which there is an ongoing programme for "banking union", which includes a Single Supervisory Mechanism for banks and an EU-wide directive as to how failing banks should be dealt with.

This is now not considered to be enough. There has been a proposal floated recently for an EU-wide Deposit Insurance Scheme, to replace the national level ones already in existence. This proposal is transparent: German taxpayers could be asked to reimburse depositors in failed Italian banks.

Another plan has been floated, to create so-called Sovereign Bond-Backed Securities and issue €1.5 trillion of them: approximately the amount of the TARGET2 imbalances. The viability of "SBBS" requires the backing to be for 70% with bonds issued by countries like Germany, Netherlands and Finland, 20% from Italy and Spain, and only 10% from Cyprus and Greece. The TARGET2 imbalances, however, are 80% Italy and Spain and 20% from Cyprus and Greece. SBBS only succeeds if there is a debt transfer from the Periphery onto the Centre – the same as a wealth transfer in the opposite direction.

And so this is the place that it comes to: the full completion of the Euro.

The steps required to achieve that are relatively few, and they may seem incremental to the many steps that have been completed as part of Economic and Monetary Union so far.

What they come down to, however, is completing a nation state with one set of taxpayers responsible for the debts of the state and the subdivisions of it, and backing a single lifeboat fund for depositors into any bank in that state.

These are enormous steps but may be all that can rescue to Eurozone and stabilise it at least in its current condition. Whether they will be acceptable to the citizenry of the Eurozone Centre is another matter. These EU member states have steadfastly resisted any action that was in itself or might inevitably lead on to debt mutualisation.

The really difficult question for the remaining EU member states is what the alternative is. To that extent the UK's decision to leave the EU before those questions become urgent is entirely rational.

Problems exposed by the 2013/14 Eurozone crisis

Several problems were exposed by the 2013/14 Eurozone crisis

Firstly the promise made about the Euro that it would deliver price stability had been hollow. Eurozone countries that had had high nominal interest rates before adopting the Euro experienced a sharp rise in asset prices as soon as interest rates became harmonised within the Single Currency and at a low level. Cheap credit fuelled a property price boom. Investors from other Eurozone countries – no longer needing to be concerned about foreign exchange rates – borrowed and invested in Euro in the Periphery countries.

Secondly the size of banks became disproportionate to the GDP ("Gross Domestic Product") of their countries. This was not a problem confined to the Eurozone since it occurred in Iceland and the UK as well. The risk in such circumstances is that the capacity of the central bank and the government of the country to bail out banks from their own resources is too small, being broadly linked to the country's GDP.

Thirdly, the promised deep and liquid capital market in Euro had not emerged. In fact it had become a distorted capital market, pricing risk incorrectly. This issue was founded on a misconception about the degree to which sharing a common currency compelled each user state to come to the aid of another when the latter experienced financial difficulties. With this misconception in mind, investors bought into government bonds of Periphery countries instead of Centre ones, because they experienced the so-called "Bund spread" – the increase in return over the equivalent yield on a German government security. Over the first decade of the life of the Euro the "Bund spread" narrowed as the concept became entrenched that Euro government bonds all carried the same credit risk, such that the yield pick-up was risk-free. The bailouts of Portugal, Ireland, Greece and Cyprus curtailed that delusion.

Fourthly – and connected to the preceding point – the Euro was not a homogenous currency. Euro "central bank money" existed in many forms. In a country with a unitary currency – like the UK with the pound – the three forms of central bank money are free of credit risk because they all represent the sovereign risk of that country. In the UK the forms would be:

- A credit balance on an account at the Bank of England (which can only be in GBP)

- GBP note and coin issued by the Bank of England

- UK government bonds - gilts

The different forms of central bank money must be 'fully fungible': instantly exchangeable for one of the other forms at par/without a 'haircut'.

In Euro the credit risk on the notes is homogenous – they are all issued by the European Central Bank ("ECB") – but they are not a sovereign risk asset. The ECB is not acting as an agent for the finance ministry of a country like the Bank of England acts as an agent for HM Treasury. The ECB is a separate legal person acting on its own account and its shares are owned by the EU member states.

The coins sit in a twilight zone: struck by the National Central Banks ("NCBs") of the Eurozone member states, they are also a liability of the ECB.

The greatest differences sit in the government bonds and in the balances on an account held at an NCB:

- The government bonds are the sole liability of the issuer, each Eurozone member state government autonomously;

- Credit balances on an account at an NCB are the liability of that NCB as agent for the Eurozone member state government on whose behalf the NCB is acting.

These problems remain unresolved. The biggest investor in Euro capital markets is the Eurosystem itself – the ECB and the Eurozone NCBs – under the ECB's Asset Purchase Programmes. There is a shortage of risk capital, which was the main reason given for the establishment of the European Fund for Strategic Investments. Most of the Periphery countries that were affected by the 2013/14 crisis remain in financial difficulties and are over-indebted.

World Bank on deep-rooted structural issues in the EU economy

This report – entitled "Growing United: Upgrading Europe's Convergence Machine" – is self-contradictory in both praising the degree of convergence achieved and then pointing areas with significant lack of convergence. Readers can download the report themselves: here it is sufficient to lift a short quotation from the foreword:

QUOTE
For both firms and individuals a convergence machine that works for all will need to provide equal opportunities to succeed. That means every European worker needs to have a basic level of skills and a labour market that facilitates easy and secure transition from one job to another as demands change. For firms, it means a level playing-field in terms of regulation and competition and a Supportive environment for innovation and technology adoption.

Growing United argues that these are essential prerequisites to maintain and build upon the impressive results that Europe has achieved. And there's an urgency to act, before the schisms that have begun to manifest themselves are widened by the exploding pace of technological change

QUOTE
Given that this is a report by one organ of the global financial apparatus on another to which it is closely linked, it is remarkably cutting: many figures in European central banking have positions on boards and councils connected to the World Bank. One can ignore the flowery testimonials to achievements so far (real or illusory) and concentrate on the criticism: Europe – meaning the EU and first and foremost the Eurozone – is falling behind and unless it subjects itself to radical change it will face intractable problems.

This was actually the message given by David Cameron at the start of the hoped-for wide-ranging reform of the EU which would then serve as the platform for Cameron's recommendation to the UK population of continued EU membership.

He was sent away with not so much as a flea in his ear. The EU authorities are deaf to calls for change because an admission of a need for change can come with an inference of past mistakes.

Instead of undertaking fundamental change the European authorities have fully mobilised existing institutions to reflate the Eurozone economy, bringing interest rates to historically low levels. This had the effect of entrenching the problems rather than resolving them.

Reflation efforts through the European Investment Bank and the European Fund for Strategic Investments

The European Investment Bank ("EIB") has been specifically tasked with increasing its lending, both for its own account and also through the newly-created mechanism of the European Fund for Strategic Investments ("EFSI"), which it administers. The EIB is the lender of all EFSI loans. This is predominantly infrastructure lending into projects that should, reasonably directly, underpin and enable economic growth. The projects themselves and the trade enabled by them should combine to deliver economic growth.

The EIB's loans for its own account rank as secondary public sector debt, since the borrowers are regional and municipal authorities and public sector enterprises, not the central government. The EIB's EFSI loans can be equated with UK Private Finance Initiative debt: a project sponsor borrows to build an asset, and then a public-sector entity contracts to use it and pays a rental for doing so. The taxpayer is committed to the contracted rental payments by the public-sector entity. The project sponsor is the borrower of the debt and pays the debt service out of the rental payments. The loan itself does not get counted into the public debt.

The debt service for primary public debt, for secondary public debt like EIB loans, and for tertiary public debt like EFSI loans is all drawn from the same well, and the EIB and EFSI have been tasked with aggressively increasing their respective parts of the public debt.

This is in line with the agreement made between Angela Merkel and Francois Hollande in 2012 - to fully mobilise the potential of the EIB for engaging in counter-cyclical public spending:

"German Chancellor Angela Merkel added her voice on Saturday to calls to bolster the European Investment Bank (EIB) and to use EU infrastructure funds more flexibly to help spur economic growth in Europe. Her comments are part of a new German emphasis on growth-boosting measures to complement painful tax hikes and spending cuts that have triggered a political and popular backlash against austerity across the Eurozone."

Specifically the bank claims, of 2015, that "the EU bank's operations will have a considerable impact on Europe's economy, adding 830,000 jobs by 2017 and 1.4 million by 2030".

EIB's projects are meant to be for infrastructure, and the up-to-date list of recently approved projects can be found here:

http://www.eib.org/projects/pipelines/recently-approved/index.htm

There are many renewable energy projects, many programmes for lending to banks for on-lending to SMEs, and many loan programmes administered by others.

The key is the amount of new loans disbursed – from the EIB 2016 Annual Report:

- 2016 - €76 billion

- 2015 - €77 billion

It can be assumed that the loans signed are disbursed over 3 or 4 years after signature and that, over time, the amount disbursed per annum stabilises in line with the new loans signed: EIB's loan signatures have been at this level for some time, since the capital increase in 2012.

The EIB administers the EFSI, which was established to fill a perceived gap in Eurozone capital markets.

The EFSI is not a fund in the sense of being a separate legal person, but a permission granted to the EIB to borrow even more money itself and lend it out into projects either itself or through its subsidiary the European Investment Fund:

- Taking a higher risk position in the financing of the projects compared to the EIB's traditional loans, which carry a 'preferred creditor' position, a factor that is frequently cited by the EIB itself as a reason for its own creditworthiness;

- This means that the EIB has a much higher risk of loss under EFSI, because the class of finance it has injected into the projects sits far further down the creditor ladder;

- The EIB is doubling its loan portfolio but on the same capital base, and this reduces the percentage of total loans that need to be lost before the EIB capital is wiped out and needs to be replenished with new pay-ins by Member States.

EFSI is meant to enable €315 billion of new investments; by September 2016 schemes amounting to 37% of this amount had been approved, although a much smaller amount had been spent. It can be expected that the loan disbursements will be running at a rate of €30 billion per annum now, and will continue at that level for the next eight years.

- Just a small selection of EFSI initial projects:

- Toscana energia gas network and metering, Italy

- Tripla Near-Zero Energy building project, Finland

- Rentel Offshore Wind, Belgium

- Energy Efficient Buildings, Germany

- MM Water Infrastructure Upgrade, Italy

- Primary Care Centres Public Private Partnership, Ireland

- Growth Equity Fund Mid-caps, Spain & Portugal

- QUAERO European Infrastructure Fund, any EU country

- Fonds SPI - Sociétés de projets industriels, France

- BPI Employment & Start-ups Programme, Portugal

- BST Employment & Start-ups Programme, Portugal

- BCP Employment & Start-ups Programme, Portugal

- CGD Employment & Start-ups Programme, Portugal

This list contains:

- energy projects to replace fossil-fuel usage;

- money for investment funds that will make investment decisions of their own about what to do with EFSI money;

- money injected through – and at the discretion of – the four largest Portuguese banks (BPI, BST, BCP and CGD), in the same way as the EIB organises its SME Financing Programmes through the self-same commercial banks, which are the ones being propped up by the ECB;

- a distinct lack of projects whose aims are both to make money and to do something new – to make or do something for money that no-one else is doing now. That, surely, should be the aim of a "Strategic Investment".

The EIB and EFSI are financing exactly the same type of projects; in fact in many cases they are committing funds to the exact same project but at different levels on the creditor ladder. These projects are not necessarily being initiated by their sponsors solely to make money. This increases the likelihood that the debt service for the EIB/EFSI loans will have to be taken out of general taxpayer funds and not out of the project.

As a result the EIB and EFSI reflationary activity is to borrow itself and induce others to borrow, for the entire amount to be spent upfront, and for the debt service to come from general taxpayer funds.

This creates an increase in GDP upfront by the exact amount of the financing, but has a deflationary effect in the long term as funds have to be diverted from other purposes to meet the debt service.

Taking the EIB and EFSI together their annual loan pay-outs approximate to €105 billion, with the EFSI portion being estimated as being spent evenly from 2017 to 2026 at €30 billion per annum.

Eurozone GDP is approximately €11.2 trillion, so this EIB/EFSI lending is creating – artificially – an up-tick in Eurozone GDP of 0.94% per annum.

The reader will permit the anomaly that the EIB/EFSI lending is into the entire EU – including the UK – and not just the Eurozone. The rationale for the version written is:

- the majority of the money is being spent in the Eurozone;

- the overall amount being spent will not tail off but the amount being spent in the UK will, and quite soon.

The ECB's "Asset Purchase Programmes"

The monetary stimulus to the Eurozone economy (and the Eurozone alone) from the ECB has been running since 2009 in the form of its version of Quantitative Easing, which it calls its Asset Purchase Programmes or APP.

The ECB mandates NCBs – the other component of the Eurosystem - to buy bonds at a rate of €60-80 billion a month, the cash then being released into the hands of the current holder of the bond and hopefully spent on other assets in the Eurozone economy.

Monex Europe's morning report on 27th October 2017 put the then current balance of APP as €2 trillion. APP was started by the ECB in May 2009, and if it had been run consistently at €60 billion a month over the 100 months between then and September 2017, €6 trillion of bonds would have been purchased. Maturities and re-sales in the meantime of €4 trillion would account for a balance of €2 trillion. This equates to 18% of Eurozone GDP, and a net stimulus of around 2.14% of Eurozone GDP per annum ((€2 trillion/8.33 years)/€11.2 trillion).

In the week of 23rd October 2017 the ECB announced that it planned:

- to prolong APP until September 2018, instead of until March 2018;
- to reduce the monthly purchases from €60 billion a month to €30 billion a month;
- to reinvest the proceeds of maturing APP bonds.

This last statement is in many ways the most significant: it means that the balance of APP will continue to increase, because the proceeds of maturing bonds are at least €30 billion a month.

If the €2 trillion portfolio has an average remaining life of five years, €33.3 billion of bonds will reach their final maturity each month on average. The amount increases if the average remaining life is shorter, and falls if it is longer.

In other words what was announced as an apparent decrease is actually an increase, from €2 trillion in October 2017 by possibly 12 x €3.3 billion until the end of September 2018, to €2.04 trillion. This rate of increase is 2% and is higher than the rate of increase of the Eurozone's GDP.

If indeed the average remaining life of the APP portfolio is 7-10 years, then the announcement does represent a tapering-off. However, the remaining life of the APP portfolio would then represent a larger risk of loss if interest rates rise: the decline in value of a fixed-interest bond for a given rise in interest rates is magnified by the bond's remaining life.

A remaining life in the range of 7-10 years would be realistic if the Eurosystem was buying new issues. APP's objective, however, is to buy seasoned bonds from investors already holding them and to put cash into the hands of those investors in exchange for the static bond asset.

Typical APP operation and how it is paid for

A typical APP operation would involve an investor that is not in the Eurozone periphery (e.g. an investor in Germany) selling a bond issued by a borrower that is in the Eurozone periphery (e.g. Kingdom of Spain), and selling it to the Eurosystem member in the borrower's Eurozone periphery country.

If the country is Spain, the Banco de Espana buys the Kingdom of Spain bonds and settles the trade by making a TARGET2 payment to the investor's commercial bank in their account with their respective NCB, in this example the Bundesbank.

The Banco de Espana not having the money to make the payment, it borrows it from the beneficiary Eurosystem member (the Bundesbank) and thereby increases both its drawings as a borrower in TARGET2, and the other Eurosystem member's balance as a lender in TARGET2.

In order to be allowed to borrow from the other Eurosystem member Banco de Espana needs to pledge collateral to it. It pledges the asset it just bought under APP and lodges it to the order of the other Eurosystem member through the Correspondent Central Banking Model ("CCBM"). The CCBM, established when TARGET was first set up in 1999, defines the legal arrangements whereby Eurosystem members can borrow from one another against eligible collateral.

The ECB list of eligible collateral sets out all the bonds that can be offered as collateral for monetary and payment operations: there are 30,000 bonds on the list and all of Kingdom of Spain's bonds are on it.

The operation described is a typical example of capital flight: an investor in the Centre disposes of an asset of a Periphery issuer. APP has actually fuelled capital flight rather than reduced it, because the Eurosystem members have been willing to buy Periphery financial assets in huge quantity, offering investors in the Centre a ready exit route.

Combined stimulus from EIB/EFSI and ECB's "Asset Purchase Programmes"

The combined stimulus from EIB/EFSI and ECB's "Asset Purchase Programmes" amounts to 3.08% of Eurozone GDP consistently over a prolonged period:
EIB/EFSI – 0.94% per annum
ECB's "Asset Purchase Programmes" – 2.14% per annum
Total – 3.08% per annum
With annual stimulus being injected into the Eurozone economy of over 3% per annum it is not surprising that the Eurozone economy is showing growth. 0.94% of that growth is directly attributable to the EIB/EFSI borrow-and-spend policy, and we will see how this policy has increased debt levels that other EU policies were supposed to be reducing.

Who transacts APP and how it is accounted

One issue with the Eurosystem is that the ECB is small: it is the NCBs that have the muscle.

The APP operations are transacted by the NCBs. However they are being done as ECB-mandated operations.

This is important because such operations are subject to an absorption of profits and losses between the NCBs and the ECB. The profits or losses that any such NCB makes on APP are not their own, but are first allocated back to the ECB and then redistributed by the ECB out to all Eurozone NCBs in accordance with their ECB capital keys (the portion of the ECB's capital that the respective NCB subscribes).

Profits and losses are booked against the capital account held by every Eurozone NCB. Profits are distributed; losses are absorbed – of course only until such time as the capital is wiped out.

The timing is also important: the profit or loss is only allocated back when it is realised. In the case of APP that would be the point when a transaction is unwound and a bond re-sold, or when a bond matures.

There is no mechanism for the value of assets to be periodically marked-to-market and the unrealised profit or loss – residing in the books of an NCB – to be reflected in the ECB's accounts.

Build-up of overnight loans between the National Central Banks of the Eurozone in the TARGET2 Euro payment system

As it is, the results of APP and also of other sources of capital flight are reflected in the unsettled balances in the TARGET2 payment system. The balances come to reflect balances of payments over time, deriving from trade and capital flows.

These flows continue to show a strong outflow from certain countries and into certain others, all over current accounts. The 24 Eurozone NCBs hold 552 current accounts with one another for the purposes of processing cross-border payments between them for TARGET2:

- they each run 23 "Vostro" accounts in their own books for the other NCBs ("Vostro" means your account with me);

- they hold one "Nostro" account at each of the other NCBs ("Nostro" means my account with you).

The end-of-day balances on all these accounts are opaque, because they are subject to a "netting and assignment" bookkeeping by the ECB whereby the ECB re-states the original balances into one claim by each NCB on the Eurosystem as a whole, or one amount due from the Eurosystem as a whole to that NCB.

The pattern is clear: through TARGET2 the Periphery owes the Centre an amount of money that is larger than all the official bailout funds combined, those being the EFSM, the EFSF and the ESM.

As at 31st January 2018 the balances in €billions were:

Borrowers owing to the Eurosystem	Amount	Lenders owed by the Eurosystem	Amount
Belgium	19.5	Germany	882.1
Greece	57.6	Estonia	0.2
Spain	399.0	Ireland	1.8
Italy	433.2	Cyprus	7.2
Latvia	6.6	Luxembourg	195.2
Lithuania	4.4	Malta	3.7
Austria	38.0	Netherlands	114.1
Portugal	83.1	Finland	67.7
Slovenia	0.1	Slovakia	10.3
France	8.9	Non-Eurozone	4.2
Total loans	1,050.5	Total deposits	1,286.5
Net ECB liability	236.0		

Greece, Spain, Italy and Portugal owe a combined total of €972.9 billion.
Germany, Luxembourg, Netherlands and Finland are owed a combined total of €1,259.1 billion.

US interest rate policy and reduction of Quantitative Easing

US interest rate policy is now to reduce the dependency of the economy on central bank stimulus and to make the economy stand on its own two feet. Thus the Federal Reserve has a clear pathway towards the elimination of Quantitative Easing, accompanied by actual increases in their own short-term interest rate.

Central bank rates are usually set for overnight funds only i.e. they apply to the balances on the accounts held by commercial banks at the central bank. In the UK commercial banks have Reserve Accounts at the Bank of England: all banks of substance – meaning they themselves run accounts for meaningful numbers of consumers and businesses – have to be part of the Sterling Monetary Framework such that they hold a Reserve Account.

The theory is that, when the interest rate on their Reserve Account is changed by the Monetary Policy Committee of the Bank of England, commercial banks transmit the interest rate change into the wider economy by altering the rates on the accounts of their customers.

The Federal Reserve has now done this several times to US commercial banks, and the Bank of England is starting to do it to UK commercial banks. The ECB has not yet started to do it.

Where it is more difficult to control interest rates is in the longer maturities of 5 years and beyond. A meaningful part of QE and APP money was spent on buying bonds in these maturities, which had the immediate effect of bringing long-term interest rates down not least because:

- the central banks were the main buyers;

- they bought in such large quantities;

- other market participants will jump on the bandwagon in such circumstances, buy the same bonds and in size as well, because interest rates were only travelling in one direction.

Interest rates then went to very low levels, meaning a flat or inverted yield curve, but what happens when the monetary stimulus is withdrawn or tapered off and official short-term interest rates are increased, is that interest rates rise disproportionately in the longer maturities. They overcompensate on the way up for the exaggerated reduction on the way down.

This is now happening in Euro: interest rates in the 5-10 year spectrum have already risen, meaning that holders of bonds in these maturities will have lost value since the start of 2018. They may still be in profit if they bought the bonds when rates were higher a year or two ago, but if they bought the bonds more recently they will now be looking at a loss on a mark-to-market basis.

This is highly problematical for the Eurosystem with its €2 trillion APP portfolio, as will be discussed further below.

Brexit

Brexit is a simple issue for the EU finances and those of the member states:

- the UK will in due course stop making its net cash contribution of around €8 billion per annum into the "Payments Appropriation" portion of the EU Budget;

- the UK will cease to be one of the guarantors for the obligations created by the European Union in the context of the funds and guarantees it has established under the "Commitments Appropriation" of the EU Budget;

- the UK will cease to have a risk on its subscribed-but-not-called capital in the ECB and EIB, and will have its paid-in capital reimbursed.

To set against this no UK borrower will be able to access funds as a member state from the EIB, or access funds from the EFSI at all. However, the UK utilisation of these opportunities is disproportionately low compared to the value of its guarantee obligations.

In order to maintain all the lending-and-spending programmes at their current level, the other EU member states will have to increase their cash contributions into the "Payments Appropriation" portion of the EU Budget, be willing to take more risk under the "Commitments Appropriation" of the EU Budget, and replace the UK's capital in the EIB and ECB.

That is not going to be easy for them to do given all the other claims on their financial resources.

EU Fiscal Stability Treaty and membership of the Euro

While all of this is going on the EU member states are meant to be preparing to come into compliance with the EU Fiscal Stability Treaty.

The Treaty on Stability, Co-ordination and Governance in the EMU, aka the Fiscal Stability Treaty, was signed amongst the EU Member States (apart from the UK and Czech Republic) to agree to reduce the ratio of government debt to GDP to 60% by 2030, and to make such adjustments as are needed to spending to take account of additional age-related social costs that may arise up to 2050 i.e. to adjust welfare spending downwards before 2030 so that the 60% ratio can be sustained up until 2050.

The "FST" is not just a Eurozone treaty, although its aim is to converge the level of debt-to-GDP in line with the original concept of the Maastricht criteria for Eurozone membership. All the countries and more that are committed to join the Euro by treaty have also signed the FST.

There are nineteen Eurozone countries and a further nine non-Eurozone ones. The degree of alignment of a country to the Euro can be ascertained on three measures:

• Is the country's currency in the Exchange Rate Mechanism (the "ERM")?

• Has the country signed the FST?

• Does the country have a treaty commitment to join the Euro, albeit an undated one?

Nr	Country	ERM	FST	Treaty Commitment for Euro
20	Poland	No	Yes	Yes
21	Romania	No	Yes	Yes
22	Hungary	No	Yes	Yes
23	Bulgaria	No	Yes	Yes
24	Croatia	No	Yes	Yes
25	Denmark	Yes	Yes	No
26	Sweden	No	Yes	No
27	UK	No	No	No
28	Czech Republic	No	No	No

Only the Czech Republic and the UK have not signed into any of these measures. Five Eastern European countries are in the FST and committed to join the Euro at some stage. Sweden and Denmark have signed the FST but have no commitment to join the Euro, although the Danish krone is the only currency in the ERM.

One of the contentions of this paper is that non-Eurozone countries will shortly be prevailed upon to fix their date for joining. The above chart proves that the European Commission is well-positioned to railroad them in an obvious order:

1 The position of the five Eastern European countries is clear: they are all but in;
2 Denmark's position has been to adopt complete voluntary convergence
   by signing the FST and leaving its krone as the sole currency in the
   ERM, so it has committed itself and can be muscled in;
3 Sweden's position maintains a fig leaf of autonomy, but its monetary policies are
   also to maintain a fixed exchange rate between the SEK and the Euro, and to have
   the exact self-same interest rate as the ECB. If Denmark goes, Sweden will go;
4 The Czech Republic's position outside the Euro will be untenable
   once all the seven other countries have been muscled in.

Current Debt/GDP ratios of EU Member States for the purposes of FST compliance

While the FST states a compliance date of the end of 2030, it is perfectly credible – and acceptable - that there could be some slippage in the FST end dates, as long as member states are on the right trajectory by the late years of the 2020s: for our calculations we have allowed for slippage until 2032. Some countries are already compliant or well on track.

But for those not on track there is even a first hurdle to be jumped now: to deliver a fiscal surplus on today's public spending budget such that there is money available to pay down the national debt. Those that are not on track in general have current fiscal deficits i.e. their public debt is actually growing. This could be permissible if the country was emerging from recession with high GDP growth and in possession of reliable projections that fiscal surplus of 5-6% of an expanded GDP would be available to pay down public debt nearer to 2032, a debt that by that time would have reduced as a percentage of GDP.

The problem is that this is not the scenario that is facing the countries that are not track. The scenario is of fiscal deficit and weak GDP growth, even after several years of austerity and even with the extensive ECB/EIB/EFSI stimulus.

The countries off track are broadly the same ones that are large debtors in TARGET2.

The key figures as of February/March 2018 in € billions are:

	National Debt	GDP	Debt/GDP now	Fiscal surplus	Surplus/ GDP	Debt/GDP end 2018
Belgium	456	441	103%	-6	-1%	105%
Germany	2,120	3,259	65%	26	1%	64%
Estonia	2	23	9%	0	0%	9%
Ireland	203	292	70%	-1	0%	70%
Greece	319	182	176%	-3	-2%	178%
Spain	1,152	1,179	98%	-34	-3%	101%
France	2,226	2,295	97%	-65	-3%	100%
Italy	2,266	1,724	131%	35	-2%	133%
Cyprus	19	19	101%	0	0%	100%
Lithuania	17	42	42%	0	0%	41%
Latvia	10	27	39%	0	0%	40%
Luxembourg	13	57	23%	0	0%	23%
Malta	6	11	54%	0	0%	54%
Netherlands	419	740	57%	4	1%	56%
Austria	289	374	77%	-3	-1%	78%
Portugal	245	192	127%	-3	-1%	128%
Slovenia	32	43	75%	0	0%	75%
Slovakia	43	85	51%	-1	-2%	52%
Finland	141	226	62%	-2	-1%	63%
	9,979	11,210	89%	-121		

These are drawn from the specialist website debtclockseu.com and, although the figures alter constantly, they can be taken as a reasonable snapshot.

The final column is what each country's Debt/GDP ratio will be at the end of 2018 given their debt, now, their GDP now, and their projected fiscal surplus/(deficit) during this year.

It then follows on that, over the subsequent 14 years starting in 2019 until and including all of 2032, the deficit countries that also have a Debt/GDP above 60% must create a fiscal surplus sufficient to reach the FST target. The only plausible way to model this simply is to project that the debt reduction take place in a straight line from 2019 to 2032 and is based on an assumed static GDP. Of course this gives a relatively gloomy picture but only relatively: in many cases even a model projecting GDP growth of 2-3% would make the attainment of the FST goals prohibitively difficult, and the efforts needed to hit the FST target would choke off the GDP growth.

We can then extrapolate the size of the task confronting each non-compliant country as percentages of current GDP:

- Total reduction in national debt needed to comply with FST;

- This reduction expressed on an annual basis as a straight line over 14 years;

- The alteration in the current fiscal surplus/deficit required to achieve FST compliance on this basis.

	Total FST reduction/ GDP	Per annum reduction/ GDP	Turnaround of fiscal balance needed, if any
Belgium	45%	3%	4%
Germany	4%	0%	--
Estonia	--	--	--
Ireland	10%	1%	1%
Greece	118%	8%	10%
Spain	41%	3%	6%
France	40%	3%	6%
Italy	73%	5%	7%
Cyprus	40%	3%	2%
Lithuania	--	--	--
Latvia	--	--	--
Luxembourg	--	--	--
Malta	--	--	--
Netherlands	--	--	--
Austria	18%	1%	2%
Portugal	69%	5%	6%
Slovenia	15%	1%	2%
Slovakia	--	--	--
Finland	3%	0%	--

We can see that countries like Germany and Finland have a nominal problem that is trivial in practice.

We can see that the turnaround hurdles for Ireland, Cyprus, Austria and Slovenia are manageable and could possibly be eliminated by future GDP growth.

But the hurdles for the other countries simply cannot be met: these are Greece, Italy, Portugal, France, Spain and – arguably - Belgium.

A delay of even one year in achieving the full turnaround from the current position makes the incline even steeper. It should come as no surprise that the incline for Italy, Portugal, Spain and Greece is already very steep. That France is in no better position than Spain could come as a shock, as will the fact that Belgium is far worse positioned than Ireland.

One might ask what happened to the Maastricht convergence criteria. These figures suggest that, whatever convergence was achieved against those criteria in the run-up to the creation of the Euro and to other nations' subsequent joining, has been undone by the way in which the Eurozone economy has behaved since.

Concerns of TARGET2 lender NCBs on gross amount and on Correlation Risk

Lender NCBs in TARGET2 have become concerned at the gross amount of their exposure in the system, and about the nature of the credit risk they are taking.

The loans are made from one NCB to another, on the current accounts they hold with one another, and are made on a collateralised basis i.e. the lender holds as security from the borrower a collateral that covers the amount of the loan plus a safety margin.

The NCB of Ireland, for example, will place collateral in the form of bonds of the Republic of Ireland i.e. bonds of the sovereign government as whose agent it acts and which is responsible for its debts anyway.

Allowing the NCB of Ireland to run an overdraft secured on bonds of the Republic of Ireland is – for the lender – the perfect example of Correlation Risk: the collateral for a loan represents the same credit risk as the loan itself. Basel III took pains to expose Correlation Risk at commercial banks and have it addressed: loans with correlated collateral have now to be recorded as unsecured.

TARGET2 balances – overdrafts of other NCBs at the Bundesbank on their vostros or credit balances on the Bundesbank's nostros at other NCBs - are liabilities towards the Bundesbank of the sovereign governments behind the NCBs:

- the overdrafts on the vostros are secured with bonds of the sovereign government behind the borrower NCB;

- the sovereign government behind the respective NCB is the obligor of credit balance on a nostro at its NCB, because the NCB is simply acting as the government's agent.

In this way the TARGET2 imbalances represent loans to the sovereign governments of other EU Member States, and ones in addition to those sanctioned in the context of the various official stability mechanisms (EFSM, EFSF and ESM).

Concerns of TARGET2 lender NCBs on current wealth transfer

The current ECB deposit facility rate is -0.40% per annum:
https://www.ecb.europa.eu/stats/policy_and_exchange_rates/key_ecb_interest_rates/html/index.en.html

This is the rate that Eurosystem members – the ECB and the NCBs – pay and receive on balances left overnight on their accounts with one another.

The Bundesbank, in depositing €882 billion for one night into the Eurosystem, pays out €9,800,000 for the privilege.

The Banca d'Italia, in borrowing €399 billion for one night in the Eurosystem, is rewarded with "negative debit" interest paid to it of €4,433,333.

This is a wealth transfer out of the Eurozone Centre to the Periphery.

Non-performing loans in the banking systems of the Periphery

Now we come to another intractable problem in the Eurozone Periphery: the Non-Performing Loans ("NPLs") that the commercial banks have on their books.

Italy is highest profile country with this problem. Italian banks have in the past admitted to holding €360 billion of NPLs, equivalent to 17% of their balance sheets. This 17% reflected the value assigned to these loans at the time, which may not have been their original and full face value.

The two issues here are the valuation of the NPLs and the amount of capital to cushion losses.

Italian banks have adopted the following phraseology:

Term	Meaning
Gross book value (or Gross Exposure)	The contractual amount of the loan, meaning the principal amount upon which interest is calculated, also known as the face value
Carrying Value (or Net Book Value)	The value at which the contractual amount of the loan is held in the bank's balance sheet, after any write-downs have been applied
Write-down	A reduction in the value of the loan in the bank's balance sheet, compared to the contractual amount

Both the Carrying Value and the Write-down can be expressed both as a percentage and as an absolute amount. The percentages are easier to follow. The problem has been in the past that the Write-down percentage has been too low, leading to the Carrying Value percentage being too high. The key piece of data that is absent is a benchmark of the recoverable value of each loan that has fallen into the NPL category, without which the Carrying Value is little better than guesswork.

Any Write-down is an expense to the Profit&Loss Account, reduces or eliminates profits, and then eats into Capital.

According to the European Banking Authority, as of June 2016, Italian banks were 97% leveraged, i.e. only 3% of their balance sheets were funded with Capital and 97% with Debt. If 17% of the balance sheet is NPLs, the bank is only solvent if 14% of the 17% NPLs are recovered, a recovery rate of 82% of their then Carrying Value.

Such a recovery rate seems optimistic but its veracity is entirely dependent upon the Carrying Value and the Write-downs already applied. Once again one must draw attention to the lack of proven external benchmarks for the recoverability of NPLs, in the absence of which the Carrying Values are guesswork.

Another way of looking at it is that the Italian banks have made the Write-downs they could afford.

With 3% of capital and 17% of NPLs held at untested Carrying Values, the banking system was arguably insolvent and should have been resolved en masse in line with the EU's Bank Recovery and Resolution Directive.

This directive has in practice proven to be unusable and for political reasons. When Banca Monte dei Paschi di Siena ("BMPS") ran into difficulties, it was deemed impossible to cancel the investments of the shareholders as the Directive dictated, since many shareholders were Italian retail investors. Instead the Republic of Italy has borrowed an extra €20 billion itself to shore up the books of BMPS and also supported it in less overt ways.

Two other banks that failed – Veneto Banca and Banca Popolare di Vicenza - were resolved by their being "sold" to Intesa SanPaolo with overt state support of €5 billion in cash and less overt state support of €12 billion in guarantees. Both banks had been deemed systemically important as they were supervised within the EU Single Supervisory Mechanism. But this was reversed by the Single Supervisory Board, allowing the matter to be dealt with under local Italian legislation. In this case a "white knight" was brought onto the scene, a solution not contemplated in the Directive.

Then there was the problem of Unicredit, with over 21% of its loans in Italy classed as NPLs at one stage in 2016, and a pan-European bank through its network of acquisitions in Germany, Austria and Central & Eastern Europe. The Italian bank showed in its 2016 balance sheet that €54 billion of its €252 billion of loans were NPLs, albeit that it had moved in late 2016 to improve this situation.

This bank undertook a major clean-up operation of its balance sheet in late 2016, in preparation for a recapitalisation via a rights issue in early 2017. The clean-up involved an €8 billion Write-down on NPLs to reduce their Carrying Value to what Unicredit deemed to be a more realistic reflection of their recoverability.

€3.5 billion was applied to a portfolio of NPLs to be sold off (referred to as the FINO project) and €4.5 billion to a portfolio of NPLs to be retained (referred to as the PORTO project).

These Write-downs reduced the Carrying Value of the FINO NPLs to approximately 13% of Gross Book Value, and they reduced the Carrying Value of the PORTO NPLs – all of the NPLs remaining on the balance sheet of Unicredit SpA - to approximately 43% of their Gross Book Value.

The FINO portfolio was earmarked to be sold off in line with the template for "market-based securitisation" of NPLs.

Template developed in Italy for "market-based securitisation" of NPLs

In 2016 Italy's government committed to a path that they termed the "recapitalisation" of the Italian banking system, using the system's own resources and so-called "market-based" transactions.

Unicredit would undertake the latter and then be able replenish the former via a rights issue.

These "market-based" transactions followed a template under which the subject bank would create a Special Purpose Company and sell off its NPLs to it. The purchase price of the NPLs would be raised by the Special Purpose Company issuing three series of bonds, or Floating Rate Notes ("FRNs").

The three series of bonds created a typical "creditor ladder", with only a very small amount of equity in the Special Purpose Company. The series lower down the creditor ladder acted as "credit enhancement" for the series higher up, enabling the higher series to obtain favourable credit ratings from rating agencies.

Indeed the rating on the series at the top of the creditor ladder should be favourable enough for that series to be admitted to the ECB's eligible collateral list, enabling the owners of that series to borrow against them at the ECB's deposit facility rate is -0.40% per annum. If a large amount of that series could be created – e.g. €86.4 billion – the Italian banking system could obtain an annual wealth transfer from the Eurosystem of €345 million.

The creditor ladder was composed as follows in the template:

The Series "A" FRNs had first claim on all monies recovered from the NPL portfolio. The amount of Series "A" FRNs should be 80% of the total.

The Series "B" FRNs had second claim, and would only receive money if the claims of the holders of the Series "A" FRNs had been met in full. The amount of Series "B" FRNs should be 10% of the total.

The Series "C" FRNs had the final claim, and would only receive money if the claims of the holders of the Series "A" and Series "B" FRNs had been met in full. The amount of Series "C" FRNs should be 10% of the total.

A special purpose investment fund was established, called the Atlante II Fund, to subscribe to all issues of Series "C" FRNs issued by the special purpose securitisation companies established by each Italian bank in turn.

Atlante II was established and funded by the Italian banks themselves with no expectation that they would receive any money back at all:

- the investment of each bank the investment of each bank in Atlante II was small, but added up to a good amount in aggregate;
- the investment of each bank the investment of Atlante II into each bank's Special Purpose Company was small – a small cushion which had the effect of making the holders of the Series "A" and "B" notes in each transaction more likely to receive their capital and interest payments;
- the investment of each bank if Atlante II's investment into each Special Purpose Company could be Series "C" FRNs of just 10% of the Carrying Value of the NPLs bought from each bank, and the Carrying Value was 30% of the Gross Book Value, then – by a leverage effect - €1 million of investment from Atlante II could remove €10 million of Carrying Value and €30 million of Gross Book Value of NPLs from Italian banks' balance sheets.

If there were €360 billion Gross Book Value of NPLs in the banking system, and these were held at a Carrying Value of €108 billion, it would only require €10.8 billion from Atlante II to clean them all out. €10.8 billion divided over 30 banks would work out to around €360,000 per bank, more for the bigger banks and less for the smaller ones, but a very manageable amount in total.

80% of the Carrying Value of €108 billion is the same €86.4 billion referred to above as the total amount of Series "A" FRNs to be created across the entire sector and refinanced at the Eurosystem at a negative rate of interest.

Failure in practice of this template because of NPL valuation

If 10% of the purchase price of the NPLs was to be raised from Atlante II, the remaining 90% was to be raised:

1. 80% from the selling bank itself: the bank that sold the NPLs received the entire Series "A" FRNs, on which the payments were guaranteed by the Republic of Italy. This was the meaning, for example, of the state support in the form of €10 billion of guarantees offered to Intesa SanPaolo for acting as a "white knight" towards Veneto Banca and Banca Popolare di Vicenza;

2. 10% from third-party investors.

Once the selling bank had decided to offload the NPLs in this way, it had to reduce their Carrying Value to 30%, sell the NPLs for that price, and receive back 80% of that price in the form of the Series "A" FRNs and 20% in cash, leave it all square in Profit&Loss terms.

- Then it already enjoyed two advantages with one to follow:

- The Series "A" FRNs, guaranteed by the Republic of Italy, could be held with zero capital against them;

- These FRNs counted a "high-quality liquid asset" for the purposes of computing the bank's liquidity ratios;

- In due course these FRNs were to be rated and go onto the ECB eligible collateral list, enabling them to be borrowed against at -0.40% per annum.

The transaction counts as a form of round trip for the selling bank. They are commercially at almost the same risk/return position as before, although their accounting situation was much improved.

The holders of the Series "C" FRNs were obtaining their advantage by acting cooperatively to clear out the NPLs of the entire Italian banking system: they had no aspiration to receive any financial returns from the FRNs they purchased.

The sole party entering the picture to take more risk than they were doing before, and needing to earn a commensurate return, were the holders of the Series "B" FRNs: the third-party investors.

They regarded the portfolios of FRNs as over-valued at 30% of Gross Book Value, and while one deal was done at that level for Banca Popolare di Bari, the next deal that came along rendered the template unviable.

This was the FINO transaction for Unicredit.

The problem was that the banks had made the Write-downs they could afford, not ones dictated by a reliable benchmark of the recoverable value of each loan.

Unicredit even invested in a portion of the Series "C" FRNs itself to get the deal away, and this was at a Carrying Value of below 13%, not 30%. Even then, the rating agencies have not yet rated the Series "A" FRNs at the level needed for them to be admitted to the ECB list of eligible collateral.

FINO proved that the Carrying Value of the FINO portfolio was overvalued at 13% of Gross Book Value, and it also put a major question mark against the valuation of the PORTO book: the valuation of the remainder of Unicredit's NPLs which were held on the balance sheet at 31/12/16 at 43% of Gross Book Value.

It now turns out that three assumptions made at the time of the Unicredit rights issue may not have been correct:

1. That the FINO project related to the NPLs that were at the bottom of the barrel;

2. that the FINO project would totally clear out this worst tranche of NPLs owned by Unicredit and held under the title "Bad Exposures";

3. that the PORTO write-down would be applied to NPLs held under the two other titles as "Unlikely to Pay" and "Non-performing and Past Due".

It now appears to be the case that, while the FINO portfolio was indeed composed of NPLs held as "Bad Exposures", the FINO project did not clear that tranche out.

Indeed, it is possible that it was the PORTO write-down that was applied to the very worst "Bad Exposures" at the bottom of the barrel, and that:

- Unicredit is still holding those NPLs, albeit at lower Carrying Values;

- The FINO portfolio - not at the bottom of the barrel and possibly of better quality than the PORTO book - still only attracted a market price of around 13%;

- If that is the case then the PORTO book is highly overvalued on Unicredit's books at 43%.

We await the 2017 Unicredit annual report for further enlightenment.

What counts as an NPL and what does not

The classification mechanism for a loan to be booked as an NPL raises questions about the full recoverability of loans booked as Performing.

Unicredit recognises three categories within NPLs:
- Bad Exposures
- Unlikely to Pay
- Non-performing and Past Due

By inference, if "Unlikely to Pay" is unlikely to pay, the lower category of "Bad Exposures" is almost certain not to pay. The FINO portfolio came entirely from "Bad Exposures", which is why a valuation of 13% was a marginal overvaluation.

"Non-performing and Past Due" means broadly that 90 days have passed since a scheduled payment was missed. This is not the same as 90 days having passed since the last payment was received, but means that 90 days have passed since a trigger event occurred.

For example, if it is a loan on overdraft at a German bank, the process starts when a customer has been in overdraft for 30 days in succession without ever coming into credit, if there is no "credit contract" and if the amount is over €1,000. A trigger is flipped at that point and the further day-count of 90 days begins.

If, after those further 90 days, the account has not once come into credit, the bank must claim insolvency under local law, in accordance with Art 178 of the EU bank capital adequacy directive. The overdraft must then be recorded as "Non-performing and past due".

The trigger can be delayed or the clock set back to zero if it can be arranged that the account comes into credit even for one day, likewise if a credit contract is put in place when none was there before.

The concern is that loans in the lowest levels of "Performing" such as "Past due" are being artificially held there in order that they not drop into the category "Non-performing and Past due": note that a loan can be "Past due" but that this does not automatically mean it is also "Non-performing".

Techniques to stop a loan dropping into "Past due" are known by the term "Forbearance", and the typical one is the capitalisation of interest, adding it to the principal instead of asking the borrower to pay it. The justification for this is usually found in collateral that is assessed as exceeding the value of the loan, albeit that the collateral may not be attachable, and/or that there is no third-party valuation of the collateral.

Capitalisation of interest may not even be necessary when the base rate for calculation of interest is -0.40% per annum. A credit contract stating cost-of-funds as this base rate and adding a 0.40% margin enables the loan to be recorded as "current" even if the borrower can not manage to bring about any debt service from their own resources. They do not need to: the all-in loan rate is 0%.

Thanks to such techniques the loan balance never gets recorded as "Non-performing and past due", even if it is suspected or actually palpably obvious that the borrower cannot repay the principal, and/or that any security for the overdraft is either not attachable, or is worth far less than the overdraft, or represents the same credit risk as the borrower itself.

Eurozone companies with very low Interest Cover who cannot sustain a rise in interest rates – "zombie companies"

It has become a major concern that the combination of very low interest rates and the accounting/forbearance techniques practiced by banks has created a class of loan that is recorded as "Performing" but will only remain so if interest rates remain at low levels, when in fact they are starting to rise.

These borrowers are referred to as "zombie companies": they cannot afford debt service and would have gone bankrupt in times of normal interest rates, whereas they have survived and distorted the economy, acting as a drag on productivity.

This article gives a perfect summary:

https://www.zerohedge.com/news/2018-03-06/europes-zombies-brace-mass-extinction-2019

"Last July, 9% of Stoxx 600 companies were zombies. In our view, **a combination of easy monetary policy and bank regulatory forbearance had allowed these issuers to "live another day", when in normal times they would have defaulted.**"

"In a year where ECB balance sheet growth will likely be over, the chart below implies that the liquidity support for zombie companies will fall away. **And other things being equal – just** as was the case in late 2011/early 2012 – the number of "zombies" will decline through the process of higher default rates in Europe."

In other words there is a latent portfolio of NPLs that will add itself to recorded NPLs in the near future. Italy has the most high-profile NPL problem but it is far from alone. Cyprus, Greece and Spain follow close behind.

Italian election result as against the need for even greater austerity

Now we have an Italian election result that rejects austerity, while the fiscal drivers are towards sharpened austerity (Fiscal Stability Treaty compliance, overindebtedness generally).

One small crumb of comfort is that the TARGET2 debts of Italy probably are not in addition to Italy's public debt. The supposition is that the Banca d'Italia is buying Republic of Italy bonds under APP and then offering them as collateral in TARGET2, such that the Republic's debt is not increased.

However, at the same time the EIB and EFSI have been increasing the levels of Italy's secondary and tertiary public sector debt, and there are many lines of Italian bonds on the ECB eligible collateral list that are not the sovereign borrower. The make-up of the APP portfolio is not public knowledge. It is not possible for an external commentator to define the total amount of debt drawing its service from the single well of Italian business and private taxpayers.

Policy shift of the ECB against prolongation of Quantitative Easing and towards higher interest rates

The ECB has recently signalled a break with the policies it has been pursuing over the last 9 years:
https://www.telegraph.co.uk/business/2018/03/08/bundesbank-back-charge-ecb-sending-shivers-italy/?WT.mc_id=tmg_share_li

This is a clear signal towards a tapering-off of support, in parallel with which there have been actual interest rate rises in Euro. Germany's borrowing costs rose to 0.75% in the early part of 2018, which was a doubling, off the low base of 0.375%. This is in the maturity range 5-10 years, beyond the explicit control of the ECB.

ECB implicitly controlled long-term interest rates in Euro over the past 9 years through its APP: by being the biggest buyer, of large amounts and consistently over a long period. Its actions in the marketplace brought the rates down, but it is less easy to exercise such a degree of control when interest rates are rising.

The technique to slow rate rises would be for the ECB to continue to buy, but then it positions itself like the Bank of England on "Black Wednesday", 16 September 1992, when John Major's Conservative government was forced to withdraw the pound sterling from the European Exchange Rate Mechanism (ERM) after it was unable to keep the pound above its agreed lower limit in the ERM. The penalty for the UK exchequer was considerable.

Or the ECB could intervene selectively to punish speculation, for example by buying large amounts from perceived speculators who are expecting prices to fall. The ECB would then continue buying up until the settlement date, at which point the speculators have to cover their short positions at higher prices and are given a bloody nose, at the same time as causing a technical reversal of the falling prices.

This can also be an expensive technique as the ECB would need to unwind its own positions and into a market on a downward trend.

In all of this the ECB's resources are circumscribed by the Eurosystem structure: it is the NCBs and not the ECB who have the major resources. They will now be holding the €2 trillion APP portfolio, of which a meaningful proportion must have been purchased during the years when interest rates were already low and flatlining. This means that the bonds-in-portfolio would have had a re-sale value as at 31/12/17 near to the price they were purchased at.

Only bonds purchased 3 or 4 years ago and with a remaining life at that time of 5-10 years will be in portfolio at a price lower than their current re-sale value, meaning that the owner has an unrealised mark-to-market profit.

Mark-to-market losses on the Eurosystem's APP portfolio

For bonds purchased more recently there will be no unrealised gain, only the possibility of a loss. This loss will remain a mark-to-market loss as long as the bond is held to maturity, pays all the interest coupons along the way and then pays out the final coupon and the full principal at the end.

The potential loss for the ECB on a mark-to-market basis is very high, given the quantum involved and remembering that, while it is the NCBs that have bought the APP portfolio, they have done so at the ECB's risk.

If we model an original 10-year bond with a 2% coupon that an NCB bought 2 years ago under APP with 7 years remaining, when the Yield to Maturity ("YTM") was 1%, then for €100,000 nominal the NCB would have paid €106,728.19. We assume for convenience that all the purchases and sales are made directly after the annual coupon was received by the then-current owner. The NCB has received two interest coupons of €2,000 each in the meantime: one year after purchase and now two years after purchase.

Were the YTM to be the same now with 5 years remaining, the ex-coupon price would be €104,853.43, but if the YTM had increased by 10 basis points to 1.1%, the bond's price would fall to €104,355.23.

Thus the bond loses €498.20 in value for every €100,000 of nominal owned, given a 10 basis point per annum rise in YTM. This becomes €4,982,020 for every €1 billion of nominal.

The NCBs have been buying €60 billion per month under APP, and we use that figure as an anchor point to extrapolate over one and three years.

We start by calculating the potential losses on one month's APPs of €60 billion of 5-year bonds, and then scale up:

Basis point loss per annum	Adverse price movement	On €60 billion – 1 month	Loss on 1 year's APP	Loss on 3 years' APP
10	0.498%	€299 million	€3.59 billion	€10.7 billion
20	0.996%	€598 million	€7.2 billion	€21.5 billion
30	1.494%	€89.7million	€10.7 billion	€32.3 billion

We know that yields on German government bonds have already increased by over 30 basis points per annum in 2018, so the above losses – compared to the value of the APP portfolio as at 31/12/17 – are quite plausible.

Against that we can set ECB's capital and reserves. The ECB's subscribed capital as at 31/12/16 was €10.8 billion. Eurozone members have fully paid in their subscribed capital of €7.6 billion. The remaining €3.2 billion has been subscribed by the non-Eurozone shareholders, but only €120 million (3.75%) of it has been called up and paid in. The remaining €3.1 billion is a recourse fund on the non-Eurozone shareholders, and the largest of these by far is the UK with a recourse liability of €1.48 billion.

It is not plausible that the ECB can call on the non-Eurozone NCBs for losses on APP, so the €3.1 billion subscribed-but-not-called capital is not available for this purpose.

The ECB had its 2016 profit of €1.19 billion on its balance sheet as at 31/12/16 but this is distributed, as was 2015's profit in about the same amount, so there is no cushion of accumulated Profit&Loss Account.

The only reserves are the Revaluation Reserves of €28.63 billion, comprising:

Element	Amount
Gold	€13.93 billion
Foreign currency	€14.15 billion
Securities	€0.75 billion
Post-employment benefits	(€0.20) billion
Total	€28.63 billion

The ECB's resources are thus these reserves and its subscribed-and-paid-in capital of €7.72 billion i.e. €36.35 billion in all – assuming that the values of the gold and the currency reserves are still at that level.

The conclusion is that the ECB cannot operations that risk realising losses on APP in the books of the NCBs which will then be allocated back to the ECB.

The ECB can taper off APP by stopping the reinvestment of maturities, and by reducing and eliminating the new purchases, but it cannot sell out the portfolio into the open market. It would create a mark-to-market loss greater than its own resources, and probably send the market into a tailspin as well, compounding its own losses.

In the process it would cause the NCBs to ask some very difficult questions if individual NCBs are sitting with portfolios at the ECB's risk but which are in deep loss on a mark-to-market basis:

- Should the NCB sell out its positions so as to avoid its own capital being eliminated on a mark-to-market basis?

- Would any loss so incurred be at the risk of the ECB or at the NCB's own risk?

- Is the ECB capable, from its own resources, of reimbursing the loss?

- Would it have to ask other NCBs to pay in more capital so that it can reimburse the loss?

- Can it insist on the pay-in or does it have to be agreed to by the ECB Governing Council?

- Are the other NCBs capable of paying in their shares?

Reduction of collateral cover for lenders in TARGET2

Since the total collateral pledged in TARGET2 is at least €1,050 billion – and indeed must exceed the total amount of loans – and the principle form of collateral is Eurozone government bonds, any fall in their value would diminish the value of collateral and necessitate the pledging of extra collateral.

This risk, in addition to the existence of Correlation Risk between the loan and the security, is a further reason why the lender NCBs in TARGET2 want to see the imbalances eliminated.

There is, however, no obvious and easy way of doing this such that the lender NCBs get their money back.

Existing pathway through Banking Union to complete centralisation – Monetary Union

Instead we have an existing pathway in the direction of mutualisation of obligations, a pathway that has an ineluctable logic to it in terms of what has been agreed to already, but which leads to a place that will not be at all to the taste of many Eurozone citizens.

The destination would be the creation of a single type of Eurozone government bond, which gives the holder an undivided claim on all taxpaying entities in the Eurozone.

The issuer of such a bond could not be the European Union for as long as there were EU member states outside the Eurozone. But part of the response to the current situation will surely be for the European Commission to put a date on the agreement of the countries like Bulgaria, Croatia and Romania to join the Euro, which was contained within their treaty to join the EU. The more difficult candidates will be Denmark and Sweden, who have signed part of the commitment but not all of it.

In the meantime there is a pathway towards the Banking Union aspect of Monetary Union, and gaining the agreement of Denmark and Sweden to this can be seen as a method of bouncing them to a point of no return where they have agreed to all other aspects of Monetary Union except Euro membership, and that they have agreed to all aspects of Economic Union.

The staging posts so far towards Banking Union have been:

- Capital Adequacy and Liquidity Directives

- Bank Recovery and Resolution Directive

- Establishment of the European Banking Authority and the carrying-out of its stress tests

- Establishment of the Single Supervisory Mechanism and of the Single Resolution Mechanism, under the control of the Single Supervisory Board

Not all institutions fall within the purview of all of these measures and are thus still subject to national supervision, but, now that the infrastructure has been established, it is the smaller task to expand its purview to include them.

It was possible, to meet the needs of the moment, to deal with Veneto Banca and Banca Popolare di Vicenza by exempting them from the Single Resolution Mechanism, so proving that the definition is permeable: further banks can be opted in just as easily as these two Italian banks were opted out.

The main rivers still to be crossed on the way to Monetary Union are:

- The national Bank Deposit Compensation schemes installed pursuant to the **Bank Recovery and Resolution Directive**

- The different credit risk attaching to deposits in the different NCBs, because the debts of each NCB are the responsibility of the member state government behind it

- The different credit risk attaching to the bonds of the member state governments

The last two points are essentially the same problem or, put another way, a clever solution to the last point would also solve the preceding one.

Although a lot of progress has been made towards Monetary Union, these three hurdles are the most politically contentious, because they make every Eurozone taxpayer jointly and severally liable for all public debts anywhere in the Eurozone and, to add to that, it is our belief that the European Commission (supported by member states like France) are pushing to make the terms "EU member state" and "Eurozone member state" one and the same.

In future, then, new joiner EU member states will accede to the Euro after a homogenous three-year transition period in the same way the initial Euro joiners did, culminating in a maximum six-month exercise to substitute Euro note and coin for legacy currency note and coin.

Proposal for EU-wide Bank Deposit Compensation Scheme

National Bank Deposit Compensation schemes were established pursuant to the **Bank Recovery and Resolution Directive**, to compensate depositors in failed banks up to €100,000 per depositor per institution.

These schemes have not been used so far, neither in the resolution of the Cyprus banks, nor of Banco Popular Espanol, nor of the Italian banks Veneto Banca and Banca Popolare di Vicenza.

The reason for that is simple: the schemes are unfunded and a pay-out would have to be met by the national government, for which purpose the government would have to add to their borrowing or, in the case of Cyprus, greatly increase the size of the bailout package.

This story from October 2017 gives the current status.

https://www.ft.com/content/58c9a172-ae7d-11e7-beba-5521c713abf4

The key paragraphs are:

"The European Commission on Wednesday proposed compromises aimed at ending two years of deadlock over the plans for a European Deposit Insurance Scheme, or EDIS. The plans have strong support from Paris and southern Europe but are viewed with deep misgivings in Germany.

Brussels argued that a deal should be reached on the scheme, and other outstanding aspects of the euro area's so-called banking union, by the end of next year" (i.e. by the end of 2018).

The full centralisation option and the business case for it

It is clear from the figures regarding National Debt and the pathway to compliance with the Fiscal Stability Treaty why the EDIS plans "have strong support from Paris and southern Europe".

The analogy of three rivers to cross was used above, but EDIS is the Rubicon because it establishes the principle of joint-and-several liability of taxpayers throughout Europe for a debt created in any subdivision of Europe, and with no cap on the liability of any subdivision of Europe: the only cap would be the amount payable to any one depositor in any one bank, but that is no cap at all on the total liability.

EDIS is also a convenient choice of Rubicon because it can be presented as a technical issue, and can be defended upon the back of the controls in place on banks' financial health, these being the usual list of "chocolate fireguards":

- Capital Adequacy and Liquidity Directives

- Bank Recovery and Resolution Directive

- The European Banking Authority and its stress tests

- Single Supervisory Mechanism and the Single Resolution Mechanism,
  under the control of the Single Supervisory Board

Once EDIS is in place, the final steps to full centralisation become ineluctable, and a refusal to take them illogical.

The question is why the Centre countries should accept EDIS, and the answer lies in the current predicament of the Euro and the degree to which the Eurozone member states have had their bridges burned regarding proceeding in any other direction.

Brexit can be brought into play by the "centralisers" at the European Commission.

Their arguments will be firstly that the Single Market and the Customs Union ("Economic" union) cannot work properly and be considered fully complete until all Member States have joined the Euro ("Monetary" union), to complete which there must also be a fiscal and budgetary union, and a debt-sharing mechanism.

This may not in the first instance be a complete joint-and-several liability for all government debt of Eurozone member states. Instead one or two staging posts short of this can be arranged – like EDIS - after the attainment of which the final step to joint-and-several liability can be presented as a logical next step in line with what was already agreed, and a short incremental step.

The principle of sharing some responsibility for debts of other countries has already been established within the EU Budget, the EIB and the financial stabilisation mechanisms (EFSM, ESF and ESM).

Secondly the UK will be construed as having acted as a brake on progress towards the objective, denying the citizens of the other Member States the benefits of full completion of the European project.

These elastic excuses for the failure of all of the Single Market, the Customs Union and the Euro to deliver on their promises of a uniform economic and monetary zone will be the more palatable headings under which to press for full completion than an admission of failure and an admission that the results of failure - the Euro sovereign debt and banking crisis – still exist and have been temporarily brushed under the carpet.

The European Commission's technique of gradualism has always worked in the past:

- To socialise the concept To socialise the concept of an increase in centralisation and a reduction of member state powers;
- To socialise the concept To handle the predictable push-back;
- To socialise the concept To then issue a "compromise" proposal, that centralises power but not to the degree inferred by the initial concept;
- To socialise the concept To railroad through this compromise… and then to socialise a concept for further centralisation.

By that technique the European Commission has moved the European project a very long way forward, such that the implications of a reversal can be presented as illogical, given what member states already agreed to.

Indeed, Banking Union is 90% complete – all that is needed is EDIS.

With that, Monetary Union is 95% complete – all that is needed is to finalise member state responsibility for one another's debts and in the process harmonise the credit risk on deposits in the different Eurosystem NCBs.

In other words the last step is the harmonise the forms of Euro central bank money.

Harmonisation of the forms of Euro central bank money

As stated above, Euro central bank money exists in several forms and is not homogenous: one form cannot be instantly exchanged for another at par value and without a haircut.

The most divergent form is the government debt of the different member states, the bonds representing which trade at different yields compared to the yield on German government bonds – the difference is the so-called "Bund spread".

Within the Eurosystem the Eurozone central banks treat their balances held with one another as if they represented the same credit risk whilst knowing themselves that they do not: each balance represents the credit risk of the government behind the respective NCB, on whose behalf the NCB is acting.

The coins are struck by the NCBs individually; the notes are all produced by the ECB. Both are the liability of the ECB, one of the weakest members of the Eurosystem.

The first change that is needed is in the backdrop to the central banking system:

- A revision to the Maastricht Treaty whereby the Eurosystem – the term for the ECB and all the NCBs – becomes a legal person and the ECB and NCBs become branches of it;

- This would mean that the credit risk attaching to notes, coins and balances held in the ECB and in any NCB would be the same: it is a claim on the Eurosystem, which accords with the way in which the ECB accounts for an NCB's deposit in TARGET2 now, even if the accounting does not reflect reality;

- A clearer interlinkage between the European Union and the Eurosystem whereby the Eurosystem is made the creature of the European Union in the same way as the Bank of England is the creature of the UK's HM Treasury.

In parallel the non-Eurozone Member States will be compelled to join the Euro. That will result in there being no difference at all between the European Union and the Eurozone. Member states joining the EU will be put straight onto a 36-month transition period into the Euro.

The European Union is already a legal person since the Lisbon Treaty and can make borrowings under the "Commitments Appropriation" of the EU Budget. This portion of the EU Budget is 0.26% of annual EU Gross National Income and, according to Moodys, is €40 billion per annum and in total €280 billion over the 7 years of the Multiannual Financial Framework 2014-2020.

The European Union has made borrowings, inter alia, to bail out Portugal and Ireland under the European Financial Stabilisation Mechanism.

The transformation that would be needed under the next Multiannual Financial Framework 2021-2028 would be for the "Commitments Appropriation" of the EU Budget to be expanded so that the European Union replaces the individual member state governments as the issuer of government debt.

Since the "Commitments Appropriation" of the EU Budget is a joint-and-several liability of the EU member states, this manoeuvre would apply the joint-and-several liability concept to the debts of member state governments.

By these measures the final form of Euro central bank money would become harmonised.

Debt mutualisation as a stumbling block

The steps outlined above do not have to be carried out all as one exercise. The changes to the constitution of the Eurosystem can be presented as administrative tidying up (as was the Lisbon Treaty), although the challenging part will be selling the concept of unified ownership of gold and currency reserves. The Bundesbank's gold reserves will cease to be theirs, and will become owned by the Eurosystem.

The railroading of non-Eurozone member states into the Euro can be done over a period, with Sweden and Denmark being the hardest to convince.

The trump card in the European Commission's hand is that these countries have already committed themselves over a very long period: EU membership and participation in the European project have been the cornerstones of their foreign policy and economic policy.

The European Commission's hand is further strengthened by the realities of power politics: these are all small countries, whose physical position exposes them to risks regarding a resurgent Russia. The UK is further distant, has a large domestic economy that is less interlinked with the economies of other EU countries, is a nuclear power and has a permanent seat in the UN Security Council.

But the debt mutualisation issue is likely to prove a stumbling block in the short term, namely within five years.

Two years is a realistic period to, in parallel, implement EDIS, convince the non-Eurozone member states to join the Euro and to agree the changes to the constitution of the Eurosystem.

There would then follow a subsequent 36-month implementation period for all these three measures.

This means that Debt Mutualisation cannot be taken in hand until 2023 at the earliest. Indeed it seems more likely that it will take some years to agree to and implement Debt Mutualisation such that the expansion to allow it in the "Commitments Appropriation" of the EU Budget may only occur in the Multiannual Financial Framework 2029-2035, and not in the one 2021-2028.

Were Debt Mutualisation to be achieved by 2030 or even by 2032, there would be no need for the extreme austerity required by certain member states to comply with the Fiscal Stability Treaty. Compliance could then be measured over the entire EU, with a need for much less pain in the Periphery.

Having said that, the Debt-to-GDP ratio of the Eurozone as a whole is currently 89%, and would need to be reduced by 29% through 2032, a not inconsiderable burden to be taken over by those countries currently not challenged by the prospect of FST compliance.

There are clear risks in this gameplan:

• That EDIS may not be agreed either at all or within 3 years;

• That the changes to the Eurosystem structure may not
be agreed either at all or within 3 years;

• That the bridges to the discussion on Debt Mutualisation are not laid down until much later than is needed to relieve member states of the burden of complying with the FST;

• That non-Eurozone member states refuse to join the Euro, or delay;

• That the problems of over-indebtedness of governments and NPLs in banks come to a head before this enormous debt-for-wealth exchange can be consummated between the Centre countries as receivers of debt and givers of wealth, and the Periphery as the inverse – givers of debt and receivers of wealth.

It reads as completely plausible that this is the long game of the keepers of the sacred flame of the European project.

We leave aside the measures that will be needed for the EU/Eurozone as a whole to achieve FST compliance from its current 89% Debt/GDP ratio on an aggregate basis: these can be sprung on the hapless Centre taxpayers when it is too late for them to object.

What appears to be imperative is an interim action to keep the show on the road in the short term while the bridges are laid down to the discussion of full Debt Mutualisation in the medium term.

Interim plan to create Sovereign Bond-Backed Securities ("SBBS")

The interim action that has been put on the table now is to create a new type of bond called a Sovereign Bond-Backed Security or SBBS. The plan was developed by the European Financial Stability Board and broadly follows the template of the Italian bank "market-based" recapitalisations.

A Special Purpose Issuing Entity is created and it purchases government bonds of Eurozone member states. The funding of the Special Purpose Issuing Entity is raised by its issuing SBBS in series:

Series	Ranking	Proportion	Backing
A	Senior	70%	Bonds of Eurozone member state governments that carry a long-term rating from Standard&Poors of AA- or better
B	Mezzanine	20%	Bonds of Eurozone member state governments that carry a long-term rating from Standard&Poors between A+ and BBB+, meaning they are of "investment grade"
C	Subordinated	10%	Bonds of Eurozone member state governments that carry a long-term rating from Standard&Poors below "investment grade", meaning BBB or lower

The backing is notional rather than legal: all investors in SBBS have a claim on all the assets of the Special Purpose Issuing Entity, but the terms of the SBBS Series into which an investor buys determines in which order their claim is satisfied within a typical creditor ladder:

Series	Order of satisfaction
A	First claim on all monies received by the Special Purpose Issuing Entity from all the bonds it owns
B	Second claim - only receives money if the claims of the holders of the Series "A" SBBS have been met in full
C	Final claim - only receives money if the claims of the holders of the Series "A" and Series "B" SBBS have been met in full

The current plan is to issue €1.5 trillion of SBBS, which would infer that the Special Purpose Issuing Entity buys about 15% of all Eurozone member state debt currently in issue.

The target buyers of the different series of SBBS are:

Series	Buyer	Rationale
A	Banks	High-quality liquid asset eligible for Basel III Liquidity computations; eligible collateral for Eurosystem operations
B	Investment funds	Safe long-term investment offering a pick-up in yield over buying government bonds directly
C	Venture funds	Speculative but high-yield in exchange for the investor being at the back of the queue

This is written as if it is plausible but it throws up familiar issues about the structure of the Euro capital market now:

- The perceived need for SBBS implies the absence of investment supply to meet an identifiable investment demand (unless the demand is fictitious and has been created by the European Financial Stability Board for other reasons than the ones disclosed);

- Conversely the case for the European Fund for Strategic Investments was the "missing investor" to meet the requirements for funding of projects – EFSI supplies official funds into a project so as to create a layer of "credit enhancement" for investors higher up the creditor ladder, and in doing so buys liabilities of the project that approximate to the level subordination in Series "C" of SBBS;
- The "missing investor" whose place has been taken by the EIB within EFSI is the same type of investor that would not buy the Series "B" FRNs in the Italian bank "market-based" recapitalisations at the hoped-for price, and who is targeted as the buyer of the Series "C" bonds in SBBS: have such investors come into being in the meantime?
- All in all these facts show that the promised Euro capital market has not emerged: a deep market across many types of financial instrument each offering a specific mix of risk/return, and right along the maturity spectrum.

SBBS credit risk

The credit risk taken by an SBBS investor is a blended risk of the individual credit risks of the government bonds owned by the Special Purpose Issuing Entity.

This is an approximate surrogate for a European Union bond in the case the European Union consisted only of the current Eurozone countries. If within 60 months all EU countries were Eurozone countries and became part of SBBS, the surrogate would become accurate.

In due course the Special Purpose Issuing Entity could be subsumed into the legal person of the European Union, in which case the debt service for SBBS would be drawn from the "Commitments Appropriation" of the EU Budget, and be the joint-and-several liability of all the EU member states.

In this way SBBS can act as a stepping stone on the road to Debt Mutualisation – but there are some short-term issues to be mastered first, indeed of such significance that it brings into question whether SBBS constitutes the stepping stone at all.

Make-up of the SBBS portfolio

According to the proposal the Special Purpose Issuing Entity should own bonds in approximate proportion to the Capital Keys of each member state's NCB in the equity of the ECB. These Capital keys need to be re-based to 100% because Eurozone member states only own 70% of the ECB's equity.

This table does that and also derives each member state's portion of the SBBS portfolio if the SBBS programme is built up to €1.5 trillion.

	ECB Capital Key	Re-based Capital Key	SBBS share in €billions
Belgium	2.4778%	3.5200%	53
Germany	17.9973%	25.5674%	386
Estonia	0.1928%	0.2739%	4
Ireland	1.1607%	1.6489%	25
Greece	2.0332%	2.8884%	43
Spain	8.8409%	12.5596%	188
France	14.1792%	20.1433%	302
Italy	12.3108%	17.4890%	262
Cyprus	0.1513%	0.2149%	3
Lithuania	0.4132%	0.5870%	9
Latvia	0.2821%	0.4008%	6
Luxembourg	0.2030%	0.2884%	4
Malta	0.0648%	0.0921%	1
Netherlands	4.0035%	5.6875%	85
Austria	1.9631%	2.7888%	42
Portugal	1.7434%	2.4767%	37
Slovenia	0.3455%	0.4908%	7
Slovakia	0.7725%	1.0974%	16
Finland	1.2564%	1.7849%	27
Total	70.3915%	100.0000%	1,500

The SBBS share of each member state is meant to approximate to the size of its economy compared to the economy of the entire Eurozone: the ECB Capital Key does that on a whole-EU basis through combining two factors:

- Member State GDP divided by EU GDP x 50%; plus
- Member State population divided by EU population x 50%.

Short-term objectives of SBBS

The short-term objectives to be mastered by SBBS are:

- To eliminate the TARGET2 imbalances;

- To taper off the ECB's APP programme but without booking mark-to-market losses on bonds that are re-sold prior to their maturity dates;

- To have an outlet for the re-sale of bonds held in the APP programme without the sale happening on the open market.

Mismatches between SBBS backing and actual TARGET2 debts

The major problem here is that the TARGET2 imbalances are concentrated onto member states whose bonds would sit against the Series "B" and Series "C" SBBS bonds, and not against the Series "A" bonds.

The current Standard&Poors' long-term credit ratings for each member state infer the following alignment of member states to the three series of SBBS bonds:

	S&P rating	SBBS Ranking	SBBS Series
Belgium	AA	Senior	A
Germany	AAA	Senior	A
Estonia	AA-	Senior	A
Ireland	A+	Mezzanine	B
Greece	B	Subordinated	C
Spain	BBB+	Mezzanine	B
France	AA	Senior	A
Italy	BBB+	Mezzanine	B
Cyprus	BB+	Subordinated	C
Lithuania	A-	Mezzanine	B
Latvia	A-	Mezzanine	B
Luxembourg	AAA	Senior	A
Malta	A-	Mezzanine	B
Netherlands	AAA	Senior	A
Austria	AA+	Senior	A
Portugal	BBB-	Subordinated	C
Slovenia	A+	Mezzanine	B
Slovakia	A+	Mezzanine	B
Finland	AA+	Senior	A

We can then group the countries by SBBS Series:

Series A – Senior	Series B – Mezzanine	Series C - Subordinated
Belgium	Ireland	
Germany	Spain	
Estonia	Italy	
France	Lithuania	Greece
Luxembourg	Latvia	Cyprus
Netherlands	Malta	Portugal
Austria	Slovenia	
Finland	Slovakia	

Interestingly the government debt of each Eurozone member state as a proportion of total Eurozone member state debt does bear some resemblance to the same member state's re-based ECB Capital Key.

We can contrast the assumed SBBS amount attributable to each member state, with their actual government debt, and their NCB's TARGET2 debt if any:

	SBBS share in €billions	National Debt in €billions	TARGET2 debt in €billions
Belgium	53	456	20
Germany	386	2,120	--
Estonia	4	2	--
Ireland	25	203	--
Greece	43	319	58
Spain	188	1,152	399
France	302	2,226	9
Italy	262	2,266	433
Cyprus	3	19	--
Lithuania	9	17	7
Latvia	6	10	4
Luxembourg	4	13	--
Malta	1	6	--
Netherlands	85	419	--
Austria	42	289	38
Portugal	37	245	83
Slovenia	7	32	--
Slovakia	16	43	--
Finland	27	141	--
Total	1,500	9,979	1,051

If we then apply to the figures in the above table the system of allocation into the bond series of SBBS by Standard&Poors credit rating, we would derive principal amounts for each Series as follows:

Series	Based on SBBS share in €billions	Based on National Debt in €billions	Based on TARGET2 debt in €billions
A – Senior			
Amount	901	5,666	66
% of the whole	60.05%	56.78%	6.32%
B – Mezzanine			
Amount	515	3,719	843
% of the whole	34.37%	37.27%	80.28%
C - Subordinated			
Amount	84	583	141
% of the whole	5.58%	5.85%	13.40%

Conclusions regarding "SBBS share" and "National Debt":
- The amounts in the columns "SBBS share" and "National Debt" are tolerably similar;
- However even there the Senior tranche is too small at 60% and could only be boosted to 70% by including all the countries with a rating in the Single-A range: Ireland, Lithuania, Latvia, Malta, Slovenia and Slovakia;
- Then the rating range for the Series "A" bonds has been expanded from AAA down to A-, which would imperil the Series "A" bonds obtaining a AAA-rating themselves, and gaining that rating is considered obligatory;
- The Mezzanine tranche by contrast is too big, but the options for reducing it are limited to moving all governments in the Single-A rating range into Series "A";
- This is because the two largest borrowers in the Series "B" range are Spain and Italy and they are both rated BBB+;
- The Series "C" tranche is too small but they are no options for expanding it beyond dropping either Italy or Spain into it: then it would be too big and either Italy or Spain would claim unfair treatment.

Conclusions regarding TARGET2 debt:
- The scheme is incompatible with the TARGET2 debt because the latter is concentrated on Italy, Greece, Spain and Portugal, whose bonds place them in the Mezzanine and Subordinated tranches.

What would have to happen to make SBBS solve the TARGET2 imbalances

For SBBS to solve the TARGET2 imbalances, the lender countries in TARGET2 would have to agree to issue more debt themselves so as to meet the SBBS proportions, pay the cash proceeds to the borrower NCBs, and allow those NCBs to buy back the collateral they have placed with the lender NCBs to secure their TARGET2 debts.

In effect this would be wealth transfer by dint of the lender countries indebting themselves by €1,050 billion, and transferring that to the borrower countries. The borrower countries would use the cash to buy their own bonds back and hold them in the manner that any institution can hold "Treasury Stock": it buys back its own securities, be they debt or equity, and holds them in its own portfolio. The cashflow on these securities is circular: the issuer pays out capital and interest through its Paying Agent, and the issuer receives back its portion on its cash account with the Custodian in whose books it is holding the securities.

This would surely be unacceptable to the lender NCBs and the governments behind them but we will see. It would be perceived as more than a Debt Mutualisation: it is a Debt Transfer. As such it is not a bridge towards discussion of Debt Mutualisation – it is a great leap over Debt Mutualisation and beyond.

SBBS as the large "stuffee" on behalf of the Eurozone taxpayers

The other purpose to be served by SBBS – although the proposal does not say so specifically - is to act as an outlet for the re-sale of bonds held in the APP programme without the sale happening on the open market.

APP amounts to €2 trillion face value of bonds mainly bought at the highest possible prices, reflecting the lowest historical yields. Now that interest rates are rising, the prices will be falling, showing mark-to-market losses that are:

- Significant as a proportion of the capital of the NCB that has bought them at the risk of the ECB;

- Enormous as a proportion of the ECB's own resources.

SBBS offers an opportunity for the Eurosystem to sell out its APP positions at prices ensuring the realisation of no losses, since the Eurosystem owns the APP positions and will be in a position to control the SBBS Special Purpose Issuing Entity.

The SBBS Special Purpose Issuing Entity will be a hold-to-maturity investor and so will not be concerned with the mark-to-market valuation of its portfolio along the way. All it will need to worry about is whether the portfolio is purchased at a price commensurate with the coupons it undertakes to pay on the series of SBBS bonds it issues.

By including SBBS on the Eurosystem list of eligible collateral the Eurosystem can more or less compel banks to buy the Series "A" SBBS bonds regardless of the yield.

But they cannot compel other types of investor to buy the Series "B" and "C" bonds, and especially if the investor type in mind does not exist in practice. This is a particular concern around the Series "C" bonds: the concern around the Series "B" bonds will be the yield, and this must offer a pick-up over the return that would be enjoyed by the same investor directly buying into the underlying assets.

However, the pick-up offered has to be limited because the SBBS Special Purpose Issuing Entity has to be in a position to buy the underlying government bonds at a high enough price to insulate the Eurosystem members from loss.

This is a perfect opportunity for the Eurosystem to side-step realising losses on the APP portfolio and to cram 75% of it (€1.5 trillion out of €2 trillion) onto this one investor, the SBBS Special Purpose Issuing Entity, who would be classed in the trade as a "stuffee" of grand proportions.

Since €500 billion of the APP portfolio may reach its final maturity anyway and run off, €1.5 trillion of SBBS may be sufficient to eliminate APP, always assuming that the APP portfolio is composed in SBBS-compliant proportions.

However, the more realistic scenario is that the APP portfolio will be showing significant losses by the time the SBBS structure is established, and the market appetite for the Series "B" and Series "C" bonds will be limited (for Series "C" it may be non-existent), and investors will want a yield pick-up over the blended yield available from buying directly into a portfolio composed of the same government bonds in the same proportions.

The numbers will not work unless:

- Just like the EIB in the case of the EFSI, an authority is used to buy in to the Series "C" bonds in order to attract buyers to the Series "A" and Series "B" bonds;

- The SBBS Special Purpose Issuing Entity is allowed to buy the government bonds directly from the Eurosystem and at off-market prices, a manoeuvre only possible if there is an external subsidy into the SBBS Special Purpose Issuing Entity, or if the investors in one of the Series buys in without any expectation of a return;

- If that is to be the solution, it will be an authority that buys the Series "C" bonds, which may be reduced to 5-7% of the total, and on terms that preclude any return, a precisely similar arrangement to that upon which Atlante II functions in the Italian bank "market-based" recapitalisations.

Does SBBS solve the APP either?

If SBBS could eliminate APP it would also greatly reduce the TARGET2 imbalances, because they are intimately interconnected.

The make-up of the APP portfolio is not public, but the fact of the interconnection with the TARGET2 imbalances and the profile of a typical APP operation (see above) would infer that the make-up of the APP portfolio is along the lines of the make-up of the TARGET2 imbalances: concentrated on Spain, Greece, Italy and Portugal.

That leads then to the same place: a mismatch of the make-up of the APP portfolio and TARGET2 imbalances compared to the make-up of SBBS if SBBS is meant to be composed 70/20/10 of bonds that are AAA-AA-/A+-BBB+/BBB and below.

SBBS then appears actually not to be a step towards the kind of Debt Mutualisation needed by 2032 in order to avoid over-indebted member states complying with the Fiscal Stability Treaty.

Summary

The promises of the euro have not been delivered: homogenous and deep capital markets, price stability (including of periphery real estate assets - which shot up and then plunged), price transparency, price harmonisation. None of these has materialised.

Now, 19 years in, the euro is in the Red Zone.

The structural problems of the euro refuse to stay under the carpet. Capital flight from the periphery is ongoing and several Eurozone economies are on life support from the European authorities:

- TARGET imbalances rising, with a clear pattern of Balance of Payments support from the Centre to the Periphery;

- Italian banks' Non-performing Loans remaining stubbornly high;

- ECB Asset Purchase Programmes increasing, with €30 bn per month of new purchases and more than that in reinvestment of maturities.

Now we also have rising interest rates – which would be disastrous for the ECB Asset Purchase Programmes as the ECB is itself thinly-capitalised and an upward movement of interest rates of only 10 basis points would cause a mark-to-market loss on the APP portfolio sufficient to bankrupt the ECB.

It will also be disastrous for "zombie" companies, who can only afford their debt service now because interest rates are near zero. The debts of these companies will increase the Non-performing Loans in the banking system.

When in a corner, the European Commission will always go for more integration, and the stark fact is that the debt burdens of several Member States (at national level, in their banks, and in other public-sector enterprises) are too high and cannot be paid if the liability for them remains on a several-but-not-joint basis. It is impossible for Belgium, France, Italy, Spain, Portugal and Greece to comply with the Fiscal Stability Treaty, even if the dates are extended to 2032, or indeed even beyond, because these countries are on the wrong trajectory now and the hill towards compliance becomes steeper with every passing day.

This is reflected in the TARGET2 imbalances of over €1 trillion.

The APP portfolio is the largest holder of Eurozone sovereign debt, it stands at €2 trillion and in a falling market.

There has been no Eurozone recovery, demand for exports from China is not at the level that flattered Eurozone GDP in 2017, and the Eurosystem cannot – for several reasons – increase the level of support.

Some action needs to be taken, though.

SBBS is not that action, and the options open to the European Commission are implausible as regards both timing and substance: they presage a "panic advance" (a "Flucht nach vorne" to coin a favoured German phrase) to:

- Muscle all non-Eurozone member states into the Euro;

- Push ahead with the Banking Union and the European Deposit Compensation Scheme;

- Further entrench, through EDIS, the concept of sharing of debts amongst member states.

The European Commission can also advance plans for the harmonisation of three of the four forms of central bank money in Euro (notes, coins and balances held in Eurosystem members) under the heading of moving Monetary Union forward from 90% to 95%.

But EDIS is a form of Debt Mutualisation as is converting the Eurosystem into a legal person with the ECB and the NCBs as its branches:

- The TARGET2 imbalances become in effect Intercompany Loans rather than loans from one member state to another;

- Gold and currency reserves are moved into common ownership.

The European Commission will try to sell these changes as both administrative in nature and as small, incremental and logical steps when measured against what member states have already implemented along the road to Economic and Monetary Union.

This line may be accepted by the power elites, but will it be accepted by the populus, and what happens if it isn't?

Conclusions for the UK

The EU and the Euro must inevitably become one and the same thing: that was the objective all along. The condition of the Euro in the Red Zone offers an opportunity for the supporters of a European superstate to enforce a going forward: they cannot countenance a going back.

The material in this paper about how these supporters might recommend getting there, with what programmes and proposals, is based on the proposals that have already been floated, and on the logical alternatives or follow-ups to them. It amounts to a package after the implementation of which there won't be any EU member states positioned as the UK is at the moment.

There will be no "Member State currencies" any longer: the euro will be the sole currency of the EU. National tax rates and budgets will have to conform to guidelines set in Brussels and Frankfurt. Debt mutualisation will be the last and ineluctable step, possibly in the early 2030s, so as to exempt individual member states from compliance with the Fiscal Stability Treaty.

However, the EU's overall Debt/GDP ratio could be where it is today – 89% - high enough to warrant austerity, all across the EU, and not confined to the member states whose individual

Debt/GDP ratio needs to be reduced. That will take some explaining to the citizens of Estonia, Latvia, Lithuania, Luxembourg, Malta, the Netherlands, Slovakia and Finland.

Joint-and-several-liability will then sit behind all Euro central bank money, and the citizenry will have been bounced into complete EU integration through the introduction of the Euro in 1999 (based on empty promises), the Lisbon Treaty that created the European Nation State in 2007 (based on the deception that it was just administrative tidying-up), and in 2018/9 the further treaty to complete Economic and Monetary Union – without the UK, which neither adopted the Euro, nor is a TARGET2 participant, nor is a signatory of the Fiscal Stability Treaty, nor is a participant in the European Financial Stability Facility and the European Stability Mechanism, nor is under a treaty obligation to join the Euro, nor is in the ERM.

This is really why Brexit was an inevitability at the point where the European authorities had either to admit failure or engage in their "Flucht nach vorne".

That the UK in effect foresaw what was going to happen and decided to leave before being given an ultimatum is all to our credit: coincidentally Brexit provides the European authorities with a cloaking device to conceal the underlying failure of the European project and bounce Europe's citizenry into its full completion.

Arguably the UK stepped off the Euro bus on Black Wednesday in 1992, but has been riven with controversy ever since as to whether to get off and stay off, or to maintain one foot on it to keep trade going and one foot off as regards mitigating the detriments of integrationist policies we had no stake in.

That mitigation has itself been a failure; we have had to accept high payments, a steady stream of onerous regulation, an influx over 3 million EU economic migrants, and a plundering of our corporate tax base by the same multinationals – out of their profit-shifting bases in Ireland, Luxembourg and the Netherlands – that seem to so much have the ear of the UK's Brexit negotiating team through their pressure group the Confederation of British Industry and its supporter in the Cabinet the Chancellor of the Exchequer.

The major worry is whether the Brexit deal that is being worked out between the UK government and the European Commission and member states is a prolongation of the one foot on/one foot off arrangement we have had since 1992, or is the clear break that the UK population voted for, once they had been given the chance.

Those in favour of trade links will be happy to have kept the UK's foot on the bus. It is another matter how they will explain away to the UK population firstly the acceptance of a continuation of the detriments that is the price of access, and secondly the direct fall-out on the UK deriving from our remaining closely aligned with an organisation that is in the Red Zone for the reasons explained in this paper.

There had better be no fall-out on the UK, either from the measures needed for the Euro to survive, or from the Euro's collapse if that is what occurs.

Appendix: The credit-rating systems of Standard and Poors (S&P) and Moodys and their importance

Credit ratings are integral to the world of investments, as they act as a guide to investors as to how likely they are to get their capital back and receive the promised interest – in full and on time - if they invest in securities issued by a rated organisation.

The bellwether securities for this purpose would be:

- Commercial Paper (issued by a non-bank) or Certificates of Deposit (issued by a bank) for securities below 1-year final maturity

- Bonds or Medium-Term Notes for securities above 1-year final maturity

The bellwether rating is the Long-term rating. When the BBC discuss the UK's credit rating being "Triple-A" or falling from "Triple-A", it is this Long-term rating they are referring to. This rating is applied to securities of over 1-year maturity, and for a security which is a bond and which ranks as a <u>senior unsecured</u> debt of the issuer:

- No tangible security is offered to the investor, such as a residential mortgage or gold bullion;

- The debt would rank equal with all other unsecured, unsubordinated creditors in the event that the organisation were to go into bankruptcy;

- The administrator of a bankruptcy estate pays out creditors in groups in accordance with the rung they occupy on the so-called "creditor ladder"; creditors in each rung are paid out in full before any creditors on a lower rung receive anything at all;

- The government usually has a preferential status on the "creditor ladder" for certain debts like for unpaid corporation tax, VAT, employer's national insurance;

- Employees may rank next, for unpaid wages;

- Next up would creditors holding security, whether a mortgage on property or land, a lien on stocks, a ship or aircraft mortgage;

- Then you have the group of senior unsecured creditors;

- Below them rank any holders of mezzanine debt and subordinated debt, and at the bottom of the ladder come the shareholders;

- The percentage that a creditor group is repaid compared to the sum of their claims is usually referred to as their "pence in the pound";

- In a bankruptcy it would be normal for shareholders, at the bottom of the ladder, to receive 0 pence in the pound;

- Moodys and S&P are thus delivering, through the credit rating, an assessment of how likely it is that a creditor owning the type of bond described will receive 100 pence in the pound.

A typical creditor ladder:

Rung	Type of creditor
1.	Legally-preferred creditors (e.g. HMRC, employees)
2.	Secured creditors (e.g. with a mortgage on land&buildings)
3.	Senior unsecured creditors
4.	Mezzanine debt providers
5.	Subordinated debt providers
6.	Shareholders/Equity investors

There are many rungs or "notches" in the S&P and Moodys systems, commonly grouped as follows:

Levels	S&P Range
"Investment Grade" – a formal term	An investment rated by S&P at BBB- long-term or better, or Baa3 or better in the Moodys system. If a security is downgraded to below that point many investors are not allowed to hold it and if they are doing so, they must sell it ('dumping'). The same investor would not be permitted to invest in a new security rated below investment grade
"Junk" – an informal term	An investment rated by S&P at lower than B- long-term: this means anything rated by S&P long-term at CCC + or lower
Below "investment grade" but not "junk" – informal because the term "junk" is informal	Bonds rated between BB + and B- long-term rank as "Speculative Grade"

Terms are often misused:
- "Investment Grade" does of itself not mean AAA and does not mean 'top-quality'
- 'Top-quality' would usually be taken to mean S&P AA or better

These are all the notches in the S&P and Moodys long-term rating systems, the grouping they each fall within, and the degree of credit risk:

S&P Rating	Moodys Equivalent	Grouping	Degree of Credit Risk
AAA	Aaa	Investment	Minimal credit risk
AA+	Aa1	Investment	Very low credit risk
AA	Aa2	Investment	Very low credit risk
AA-	Aa3	Investment	Very low credit risk
A+	A1	Investment	Low credit risk
A	A2	Investment	Low credit risk
A-	A3	Investment	Low credit risk
BBB+	Baa1	Investment	Moderate credit risk
BBB	Baa2	Investment	Moderate credit risk
BBB-	Baa3	Investment	Moderate credit risk
BB+	Ba1	Speculative	Substantial credit risk
BB	Ba2	Speculative	Substantial credit risk
BB-	Ba3	Speculative	Substantial credit risk
B+	B1	Speculative	High credit risk
B	B2	Speculative	High credit risk
B-	B3	Speculative	High credit risk
CCC+	Caa1	Junk	Very high credit risk
CCC	Caa2	Junk	Very high credit risk
CCC-	Caa3	Junk	Very high credit risk
CC	Ca	Junk	In or near default, with possibility of recovery
C	Ca	Junk	In or near default, with possibility of recovery
SD	C	Junk	In default, with little chance of recovery
D	C	Junk	In default, with little chance of recovery

Glossary

Central bank money
Forms of money that are regarded as free of credit risk by the central bank of a particular country, being money that represents the sovereign risk of that country. In the UK the forms would be:

- A credit balance on an account at the Bank of England (which can only be in GBP)

- GBP note and coin issued by the Bank of England

- UK government bonds - gilts

The different forms of central bank money must be 'fully fungible': instantly exchangeable for one of the other forms at par/without a 'haircut'

Credit enhancement
Generic term for any form of security, guarantee, insurance policy or third-party undertaking that reduces the credit risk taken by a lender when advancing funds to a borrower, and which makes full repayment of capital and interest, and on time, more likely.

Creditor ladder
The seniority level of a creditor's claims in a bankruptcy. The trustee of the bankruptcy will pay out the proceeds of the liquidation of the assets in order of creditors' seniority. The first level will be paid out in full before the next level receives anything. Shareholders are at the bottom of the ladder. The amount that a certain level of creditors gets paid out as a percentage of their claims is known as "pence-in-the-pound". The maturity date of a creditor's claim has no impact on its seniority in a bankruptcy: secured long-term claims will outrank unsecured short-term claims.

Credit rating
An estimate of the ability of a person or organization to fulfil their financial commitments in full and on time, based on previous dealings

Credit rating agency
A credit rating agency (CRA, also called a ratings service) is a company that assigns credit ratings, which rate a debtor's ability to pay back debt by making timely capital and interest payments and the likelihood of default. Standard and Poor and Moodys are the two best known CRAs

EU Fiscal Stability Treaty or "EFST"
The Treaty on Stability, Co-ordination and Governance in the EMU, aka the Fiscal Stability Treaty, signed amongst the EU Member States that are part of the Single Currency – the EUR – to agree to reduce the ratio of government debt to GDP to 60% by 2030, and to make such adjustments as are needed to spending to take account of additional age-related social costs that may arise up to 2050 i.e. to adjust welfare spending downwards before 2030 so that the 60% ratio can be sustained up until 2050

European Financial Stabilisation Mechanism ("EFSM")
The first Eurozone bailout mechanism, agreed in May 2010 and involving all EU Member States. The ceiling is €60 billion; €46.8 billion is currently lent to Ireland and Portugal. €13.2 billion is available.

European Financial Stability Facility ("EFSF") www.efsf.europa.eu
The second Eurozone bailout mechanism, also agreed in 2010 but involving only the Eurozone members. It has loans out under three programmes, all fully drawn: Ireland €17.7 billion; Portugal €26.0 billion; Greece €143.6 billion; total €187.3 billion. It is a Luxembourg-incorporated special purpose company. Its capital is in the form of part-paid shares owned by the Eurozone countries, with the subscribed-but-uncalled capital callable on a several-but-not-joint basis. No new programmes can draw on the EFSF, and no existing borrowers can draw more. The ESM administers the EFSF, meaning receiving capital and repayments on its loans, paying out on the bonds issued to finance the loans, and calling the capital when needed

European Stability Mechanism ("ESM") www.esm.europe.eu
The third Eurozone bailout mechanism, also agreed in 2010 and again involving only the Eurozone members. It has a maximum lending capacity of €500 billion, of which €450 billion is currently available. It is a Luxembourg-incorporated special purpose company. Its capital is in the form of part-paid shares owned by the Eurozone countries, with the subscribed-but-uncalled capital callable on a several-but-not-joint basis. New programmes can access the ESM and the EFSM, but not the EFSF.

Eurosystem – the European System of Central Banks ("ESCB")
The European System of Central Banks (ESCB) is composed of the European Central Bank (ECB) and the national central banks (NCBs) of all 28 EU Member States. The ESCB is responsible by EU Treaty for issuance of Euro note & coin and for carrying such operations as are needed for the proper functioning of the Euro within the scope of the Treaty mandate and the ECB/NCBs' own statutes and powers

Exchange Rate Mechanism or ERM
The European Exchange Rate Mechanism, a system introduced by the European Community in March 1979, as part of the European Monetary System (EMS). Its goal was to reduce exchange rate variability and achieve monetary stability in Europe, in preparation for Economic and Monetary Union and the introduction of a single currency, the euro, which took place on 1 January 1999. After the adoption of the euro, it mutated into ERM II, a policy charged with linking currencies of EU Member States outside the Eurozone to the euro, having the common currency as a central point. The goal was to improve the stability of those currencies, as well as to gain an evaluation mechanism for potential Eurozone members. The only currency still in the ERM is the Danish kroner (DKK) whose central valuation against the EUR is EUR1 = DKK7.46038. The last one out was the Lithuanian litas (LTL) when it joined the Euro on 1/1/15 at an irrevocably fixed exchange rate of EUR1 = LTL3.4528

Gross Domestic Product

A monetary measure of the value of all final goods and services produced in a period (quarterly or yearly). Nominal GDP estimates are commonly used to determine the economic performance of a whole country or region, and to make international comparisons.

Gross National Income

The sum of value added by all producers who are residents in a nation, plus any product taxes (minus subsidies) not included in output, plus income received from abroad such as employee compensation and property income

Joint-and-several liability

An arrangement amongst parties to a business transaction, usually under a guarantee from shareholders in favour of creditors, where the creditors may recover all of their claim from any of the shareholders regardless of their individual share in the company

Multiannual Financial Framework

The MFF: the EU long-term spending plan. The multiannual financial framework lays down the maximum annual amounts ('ceilings') which the EU may spend in different political fields ('headings') over a period of at least 5 years. The current MFF covers seven years: from 2014 to 2020

Several-but-not-joint liability

An arrangement amongst parties to a business transaction, usually under a guarantee from shareholders in favour of creditors, where the creditors may only recover from any shareholders the same share of the claim as that shareholder owns in the business – shareholders are not responsible for one another's obligations

Sovereign risk

"Sovereign risk" is the credit risk of a government – the best and lowest credit risk available in the country concerned. It was thought to be synonymous with being a type of obligation that was free of credit risk, up until the Latin American 'foreign currency debt' defaults of the 1980s. After that, the definition of "risk-free" was amended from "any debt obligation of a sovereign government" to "any debt obligation of a sovereign government in its own currency". Gilts in the UK or Treasuries in the US qualify as that: in other words foreign currency obligations were not considered as risk-free but domestic currency obligations were. This definition has been undermined by the EUR, where several countries use a currency but none has the control over the tools for its management commensurate with its obligations being regarded as risk-free. To be genuinely credit risk-free an obligation of a government must be in its own currency of which it is the sole user. The existence of multiple users of a currency damages the quality of the central bank money in that currency and reduces the quality of the respective government's Sovereign Risk, which is fault line at the centre of the Euro.

Subscribed share

A shareholder enters into a contract to take ownership of a share in exchange for a consideration, normally cash. The shareholder is committed at the point of subscription, and has an enforceable obligation to deliver the cash on the due date.